# THE JOY OF PLANTING

## 101 RECIPES FOR POTS & CONTAINERS

*A STEP-BY-STEP GUIDE TO CREATIVE CONTAINER GARDENING*

WARNING:
STUDIES INDICATE
GARDENING IS HIGHLY ADDICTIVE

# ARLETTE LAIRD

Illustrations by Suzanne Laird
Photography by George Huczek

*See front cover container identification on page 3.*

# The Joy of Planting – 101 Recipes for Pots and Containers
## by Arlette Laird

Second Printing – April 2001

**Copyright © 2000 by**
**Pirouette Publications**
Site 21 – 9 – RR 5
Prince Albert, Saskatchewan
Canada  S6V 5R3
E-mail: pirouette_order@hotmail.com

**Canadian Cataloguing in Publication Data**

Laird, Arlette

The joy of planting : 101 recipes for pots & containers : a step-by-step guide to creative container gardening

Includes index.
ISBN 1-894022-41-6

1. Container gardening.  I. Laird, Suzanne, 1979–
II. Title.

SB418.L35      2000    635.9'86        C00-920005-3

Design by
Brian Danchuk
Brian Danchuk Design, Regina, Saskatchewan

Wire Pots supplied by G.M. Multi-Formes Inc. (418) 483-5430
Fibre and hanging pots supplied by Kord Products  (905) 452-9070
Plastic pots and urns supplied by TPI Plastics (518) 841-7066
Plastic pots and urns supplied by  ITML 1-800-736-4865
Steel gazebo, steel table, hangers, wrought iron basket, victorian plant
  stand, supplied by Steelmet 1-800-667-3046 or (306) 931-2885
Premier Pro-Mix soil supplied by United Horticultural Supply
  1-888-273-4330 (West)      1-800-328-4678 (East)

Formatting by Iona Glabus

Designed, Printed and Produced in Canada by:
Centax Books, A Division of PW Group
Publishing Director: Margo Embury
1150 Eighth Avenue, Regina, Saskatchewan, Canada S4R 1C9
(306) 525-2304   Fax: (306) 757-2439
centax@printwest.com         www.centaxbooks.com

# TABLE OF CONTENTS

**Cover Photo**
1 *Layer Cake, page 95*
2 *Midnight Stars, page 100*
3 *Spiced Chiffon, page 134*
4 *Limòn Sorbet, page 143*
5 *Tangy Fiesta, page 130*
6 *Peach Cobbler, page 110*
7 *Glazed Crunch, page 121*

# DEDICATION

**F**or Philomene Blanche, for whom growing snapdragons, pansies and gladiola was a necessary pleasure at a time and in a place where flower gardening was seen as a frivolous pastime.

# ACKNOWLEDGEMENTS

**T**hank you Margo Embury and everyone at Centax Books and Distribution for helping me to orchestrate this project.

Major thanks to the management and staff at Par Industries for giving me the opportunity to make my own mistakes and for encouraging me in my successes; thanks to all of my customers, and especially Peggy Green, who insisted on the best and the most varied pots – it's been a privilege working for you.

Thanks to George Huczek and Suzanne Laird, for inspiring me to do my very best so that my work could live up to yours.

Thanks also to Gerry Laird for getting me going, for having faith in my abilities and for letting me learn from you – it didn't cost me a nickel; John Van Beveren of Ball Superior for always keeping me up to date, for being objective about all the products available and especially for telling me – from the very start, "you gotta do it"; Gerald Gareau of Le Conseil de la Cooperation de la Saskatchewan for helping me elaborate a plan; and to Lisa Havlicek and Yves Aquin of La Societe Candienne Francaise de Prince Albert for sharing their computer expertise.

My gratitude and thanks also goes to my family, Grant, Christine, Bridget and Gent, who not only supported me but pitched in and helped in all kinds of ways; Alice, Julie and mom for backing me and for doing some of the dirty work; and thanks, Tom, for the scrambled eggs.

# INTRODUCTION

If you can scramble an egg, you can fill a container; if you can pour yourself a glass of water, you can water your plants; if you can add salt and pepper to taste, you can handle fertilizer, and if you can transfer a piece of cake from the pan to a plate, you can transplant a plant.

In other words, if you can feed yourself, you can handle container gardening. If you have no experience, don't start with a large meal – one or two pots will do. If you're a good gardener with lots of experience, – go gourmet! All you really need is a good recipe book!

If you don't think you have a green thumb, this book will help you develop one; if you do have a green thumb, maybe this book will give you some ideas. Either way, these recipes will be handy for planning your baskets and pots according to color and taste, putting together a shopping list, guiding you through pot filling and giving simple instructions on growing a gorgeous floral show.

Gardening in pots has all kinds of advantages. Busy people can dress up their homes and yards with very little time and effort, and we all know there are lots of busy people these days! The beginner can practice gardening without having to hoe, rake and weed – it's great for disabled people, too. Container gardening is a great way to sample plant material and risky color schemes; if you end up liking what you've got, then next year, you can use it for a whole garden plot. Best of all, for people with poor soil, you can have your garden without ever digging, shoveling or altering the ground you live on. In other words, you can have your cake and eat it too!

Pots are great because they can be moved around. If there's company coming, the pot from the back door can be moved to the front. If there's an especially favorite container planting on the deck, it can be moved so that you can see it and enjoy it from the kitchen or family room. If there's a cloudburst with pounding rain, or worse – hail, the pots can be sheltered in the garage, or even in the house. If you have a planting that gets too big for its space, just move it. You can even take your pots on a trip! In my travels, I've often seen container plants perking up trailer lots in campgrounds.

The size of the kitchen doesn't stop anyone from cooking and baking. That's true about container gardening, too; almost anyone has room for a pot or two, no matter how small the yard or the balcony!

The size of a kitchen doesn't stop anyone from using a recipe book, either. So whether you have lots of containers or just a few, use all of the information in this book. Read it from beginning to end. Even if you're an expert gardener, don't hesitate to skim over the informational chapters before heading into the recipe part. There are a few things in there about the recipes and how and why they are written up the way they are. The chapter "More Dimes Than Dollars" might save you a buck or two so it's certainly worth taking a look at. And why not keep a little summer all winter long? That's what "Preserving" is all about.

I don't know what kind of cook you are, or if you cook at all, but I do know I'm the kind of person that can't leave well enough alone. I always change the recipe – I put in less sugar, use an extra egg, put in a different spice, whatever! Sometimes it works out well and other times, not so well, but it's always edible; in any case, it's never the same and I always learn something. Hopefully, you'll get adventurous too – with these recipes – changing this, adding that. The chapter on design elements, "Cooking Secrets" can help you along. As your confidence grows you'll discover and develop your own creativity. After all, the perfect arrangement for you is totally based on your perspective, so go for what pleases you, express yourself!

There is method to the madness in the chapter Everyday Favorites. **The recipes are in the order listed in the table of contents.** The first section is **hanging baskets**; note that most of these can be used as patio pots as well – except the wire baskets, of course! The **color bowls** are all together, too, but these can be planted in deeper containers if that's what you want or have. A few recipes call specifically for **square pots** or for **rectangular containers** and then, of course, there's a large section of **patio pot** recipes – from 10" (25 cm) to 24" (60 cm) across.

Simple ingredients can make beautiful pots just as simple ingredients can make a wonderful dish. What could be yummier than strawberries and whipped cream? Strawberries alone are very good. Whipped cream by itself has very few fans. The combination of the two not only looks very inviting, it sends the taste buds zooming.

The same can be said of container gardening. It's not necessarily the individual plants that make it appealing, it's the combo. Now that you have a recipe book, start putting those combos together. Mix a bit of soil, pour a little water, add a pinch of fertilizer, transfer a few plants, have a lot of fun and keep the old KISS concept in mind; you know – **Keep it Simple Sweetheart!**

# KNOW YOUR INGREDIENTS

To be a successful cook, you need to know what you're cooking with. You need to know the difference between enriched flour and stone-ground whole-grain; what effect substituting water for milk might have; when you should be using a cast-iron frying pan or a stainless steel saucepan.

Gardening is no different. You need to know what you're dealing with. For the experienced gardener, you may get new ideas in this chapter. For the beginner, you will learn enough to get started but hopefully not so much as to totally confuse you.

The theme throughout this chapter is the same as it is throughout the book: KISS (**Keep It Simple, Sweetheart!**).

## TOOLS:

Even for the simplest of dishes, you need all kinds of kitchen utensils. Thank goodness container gardening is a lot less complicated! The tools you should have are:

- ❀ a **trowel** to dig with
- ❀ a **knife** to separate plants if they don't come in cell packs
- ❀ a **watering can**
- ❀ a pair of **scissors** (I always used whatever scissors were lying around. I once used a small pair of embroidery or trimming scissors and have stuck to them ever since – less chance of trimming off more than bargained for with these little guys.)
- ❀ If you have a number of pots, then you need a **water hose** with a good **wand** and a nozzle with a nice, soft flow, called a **flood nozzle**.

## CONTAINERS:

You can dress up a meal by using fancy dishes. The food will taste the same but it will look more attractive. The same applies to containers. Pots keep the show together but they are not the show. Mind you, a pot can be a source of inspiration. An earthy-type pot may lead you to put a herb or two into your combination, while a cement urn might suggest a more formal arrangement.

Use whatever container turns you on – from plastic, to clay, to straw baskets. Whatever you use, **what's important is the size and shape**. If you're using a pot that's 12" (30 cm) across, but only 3" (8 cm) deep, you'll be constantly watering and fertilizing, fighting pests and diseases.

I don't recommend small pots for that very reason. **I stick to pots with a 10" (25 cm) or larger diameter and at least 5" (13 cm) deep**.

If, of course, you have plenty of time and love giving attention to your plants, if you have a special pot that fits perfectly in a problem area, then go ahead and use that small pot. You know what you're getting into and are prepared to do what needs to be done.

As I said earlier, what a pot looks like is not the most important thing – **what is important is that it drains properly**; that means holes in the bottom. Putting in rocks or bits of broken clay pots helps, but if there is a lot of rain, over a short period of time, you could still end up with a mud/water garden. So, whatever size and shape – go for the holes!

Wood and clay pots look great but dry out more quickly than plastic or fiber. If you love the look, consider using an inexpensive plastic or fiber container and dropping it into the clay pot. Of course, if your clay or wood pot is very large, e.g., 16 or 18" (40 or 45 cm) then that drying out will not be much of a problem. My beef is with the open-bowl type of terra cotta pots and, as usual, the smaller they are, the worse the problem. Also, if your pot will be sitting in a mostly shaded area, drying out won't be as much of a problem as with a pot that is out in the sun all day.

By the way, a "fiber pot" is not made of heavy-duty cardboard, as I once imagined, but of wood fiber. They have that earthy look some people are looking for; like the clay pots, they breath, and their drying-out factor is somewhere in between clay and plastic.

Wire pots are used to make great balls of flowers! Planting all around the outside makes for a dramatic and luscious-looking hanging pot. Of course, with this type of pot, you're stuffing in many more plants than you would in the same-size regular pot so it will require more general care.

## SOIL:

When you make bread, the flour you use makes a big difference. If you go for straight white, you won't knead as long as if you use part whole-wheat or rye. You might adjust the amount of yeast you use and liquid; the bread will also rise differently with one type of flour than with another. The same is true of soil. It receives, stores and helps distribute the moisture and the nutrients. So, the type of soil you use makes a difference on how fast your plants will grow and how often you water and fertilize.

There are two types of soil: **Soil-Base mix** and **Soilless mix**. A soil-base mix actually uses real soil! The basic recipe is:

# Soil-Base Mix

**1 part soil,**
**1 part vermiculite,**
**1 part peat moss.**

You can use good-quality bagged topsoil or you can use your own garden soil.

**The advantages of a soil-base mix are:**

&#10087; It retains moisture quite well.

&#10087; Soil buffers the effects of improper fertilization – in other words, if you make a mistake mixing fertilizer, there's less chance the plants will burn (or starve).

&#10087; A soil mix is less expensive than a ready-made mix.

&#10087; You don't absolutely need to fertilize a soil-base medium.

**The disadvantages of the same mix are:**

&#10087; Your mix might be inconsistent. Each batch might be different.

&#10087; A soil mix may not drain well enough.

&#10087; It takes time to mix and it makes a mess.

&#10087; A pot full of a soil-base mix can be heavy to handle.

Now let's take a look at **soilless mixes**. Hobby gardeners and greenhouse growers have been turning more and more to all types of soilless mixes. One reason for this is that topsoil free of pesticides and fertilizers is getting very hard to find. Besides, the companies that develop soilless media, are very competitive which makes for excellent mixes at reasonable prices.

**A soilless mix is just that. There is no soil in the bag. What you'll find is perlite, vermiculite, peat moss (an/or coco fiber), a wetting agent and enough fertilizer to get the plants growing.**

The very best comes in large bales – which is great if you plan on making up lots of pots.

**The advantages of a soilless mix are:**

- ❀ A pre-mixed medium is the same from pot to pot as it is from bag to bag.
- ❀ Wetting agents are included in the mix so it retains moisture quite well.
- ❀ There's plenty of oxygen available for root growth. Plants really take off when planted in a soilless mix.
- ❀ A soilless medium is very light and easy to work with – no fuss, no muss.

**I have to admit, there are some disadvantages to this medium as well. They are:**

- ❀ The mix can dry out quickly – watch those windy days!
- ❀ You have no choice but to use fertilizer in a soilless medium.
- ❀ As always, you pay more for the convenience a soilless mix offers.
- ❀ Again, the advantage of a light pot becomes a disadvantage. If the medium dries out too much and the wind comes up, as it so often does, a small pot can be knocked over!

Where does **all-purpose potting soil** fit in all of this? Somewhere in between. Sure, it has soil in it, but not a whole lot, just enough to not need fertilizer in the mix. It's not as heavy as a soil mix, but heavier than a soilless mix. It has different ingredients in different proportions than a soilless mix – for one thing, there is more peat moss in it and less vermiculite. By the same token, it also has different proportions than a soil mix. All these choices do complicate things, I have to admit.

If life were simple, all you'd have to do is choose between a soil mix of your own, or a store-bought soil mix, or a soilless mix. But there are other options. For example, you can mix one-quarter to one third garden soil or topsoil into your soilless medium or your bagged soil mix. Or you can get lazy and still get the advantages of both while minimizing the disadvantages by doing what I often do: **fill your pot about one-quarter full with your garden soil/topsoil and fill the remaining three quarters with a soilless mix.** (In the greenhouse, I use sterilized, bagged black soil.)

The soilless mix helps plants take off with a boom. Then, as the plants mature, the roots reach down to the soil, where they get added nutrients. The soil, being on the bottom, takes longer to dry out and it adds weight.

If you decide to add garden soil to your purchased soil mix or soilless mix, be sure not to use a smidgen more than one-third. If you get carried away and use more, you will find that the soil crusts, that it does not have good drainage and that the pots are heavy – an especially bad idea for hanging baskets.

If you're tempted to use the same soil as last year, reconsider. A little bit of soil in a pot full of plants gets depleted very quickly. You'd be starting out with zero nutrients. If your plants had bugs last year, they may have laid eggs in the soil so you'll be infested again this year. Mind you, if you have very large pots, you can keep the bottom half of the soil and fill up the remainder with fresh stuff – but the pots must be deep enough so that the roots haven't reached all the way to the bottom.

Do what suits you best. Plants want to live and they will be happy with any of the above choices (or combination thereof). This is the joy of planting!

## WATER:

Everyone knows our body is 90% water. That's why it's so important to drink plenty of fluids, especially water. Well, plants are 90% water too! And, what can I say? Rainwater is always best for plants; unfortunately, rain dancing every day may still not turn on the heavenly showers. And believe me, plants in pots can keel over very quickly without this magic potion! So take out the garden hose!

If your water is good enough for your houseplants, it's good enough for your pots. If it's good enough for you, chances are it's fine for your plants. But, beware of the water softener. If you don't have access to softener-free water, be sure to collect rainwater whenever you can and water your plants thoroughly with it every once in a while. You have to flush out salt build-up or you will end up with unhappy plants.

## FERTILIZERS:

It would be easy to cook if you didn't have to consider nutrition. Unfortunately, if you ate rich, creamy, salty, fatty foods all the time, you'd end up in pretty bad shape! Nutrients are important to plants too, and there isn't a lot of soil in a pot. When the roots run out of food and water, they dig deep and soon hit the bottom! That's where fertilizers come in.

Ever wonder what the numbers mean on the fertilizers you buy? What the heck's the difference between 5-10-5 or 20-20-20? Here are the basics:
- ❀ The first number is **nitrogen**, for green growth.
- ❀ The second is **phosphorous**, for root growth.
- ❀ Third is **potassium**, for strong stems and roots, for disease resistance.

What's a **complete fertilizer**? That's a fertilizer that does not include a zero in the three numbers. Fertilizers worth their grain of salt include "micro-nutrients" or "trace elements". Sulphur, calcium, iron, and zinc are some of those elements and are usually included in a "complete" plant food.

The higher the numbers on the bag, the higher the concentration. 20-20-20 has a higher concentration of the three basic ingredients (nitrogen, phosphorous and potassium) than does 5-10-5. The numbers tell how much of one ingredient there is as compared to the others. 5-10-5 has one part nitrogen to two parts phosphorous to one part potassium. What else is in the bag? Compounds to help the fertilizer dissolve in water and, of course, fillers.

Have you got enough information yet? I hope not; more is coming.

A **balanced fertilizer** is a fertilizer where all three numbers are even, like 14-14-14 or, again, 20-20-20.

A **slow-release fertilizer** comes in granular form – little grains you mix directly into the soil. It does as the name suggests; it slowly releases nutrients over time. It's usually good for up to six weeks. It's very practical, but it doesn't eliminate the need for a good water-soluble fertilizer.

**Water-soluble fertilizer** is a powder and it dissolves best in warm water.

**I recommend a balanced, complete fertilizer in granular form (14-14-14), mixed in with the soil as well as a water-soluble balanced fertilizer (20-20-20) to be used later in the season.**

Here's the most important piece of information: READ THE LABEL. Don't wait till all else fails, read the instructions first and foremost. Remember, plants just want to live; reading and following instructions might make the difference between life and death for your plants!

## LIGHT REQUIREMENTS

Most gardening literature refers to the light requirements of plants as shade or sun, but the amount of heat that the plant gets is at least as important as the amount of light. Let's say you have a wide overhang on the south side of your house. Well then, you have shade, don't you, so why not grow a fuschia there? It won't work. Even though your fuschia is in shade all day long, if your overhang faces south, and is against the house, the temperature in that space will get quite hot on a warm day. Fuschias actually like light, but they really don't like heat; actually they hate being over 75°F (25°C). There you have it. Shade does not necessarily mean cool.

If it's too hot for fuschia, will heat-loving portulaca do as well in the same spot? The answer is no, because there wouldn't be enough light there, and the portulaca closes up in low light conditions, .

Well then, you say, what the heck will do well in this warm but shady location? Let's see – petunias would be fine, impatiens probably would too, also marigolds – actually quite a number of plants. There are really only a few plants that are very specific and fussy about their needs.

So we know that light has various degrees of heat. A plant on the south-east side of the house may get as many hours of sunlight as plants on the south-west side. The fact that those hours come at varying times of the day makes a big difference. The morning sun is not as hot as the afternoon sun, making for very different conditions on the two corners.

For example, lobelia would do really quite well on the south-east side, but would need a lot of water and give up on life a lot quicker on the warmer south-west side. Portulaca would be okay on the south-east corner but would lo-o-o-ve the heat of the south-west corner.

When you read up on pansies, you'll find that they will grow in sun or part shade. The truth is that they will do fine in the sun but they don't like heat, so they'll be fine in the middle of the yard but not right up against the south or west wall of the house, or along a cement driveway or any other place that will reflect heat back on the plants.

Zinnias, on the other hand, love the heat. They will grow almost anywhere but will bloom profusely in, say, a brick planter against the south side of a house. If it happens to be a cool summer, though, they won't perform the same way in the same spot as they will during a blazing summer.

That's another thing you should know; don't expect plants to perform consistently from one year to another. Dianthus will be wonderful if the weather isn't too hot, but they will want to go to seed in an extended heat wave and they may even stretch! You know what this country is like – completely unpredictable from one day to the next, never mind from one year to the next!

## PLANT MATERIAL

Recipe books that ask for ingredients that an ordinary person has in an ordinary kitchen are so much handier than books requesting all kinds of exotic stuff you have to fly to China to get!

That's why I've tried to stick with easy-to-obtain and easy-to-grow varieties that will do well with basic care and attention. The information you need to grow these varieties is included in the recipes, but if you want more, get thee to thy local library. There are all kinds of books written specifically for your region, so grab one!

Some plants that seem new to you may actually have been around for a long time; say **Dahlberg daisy** or **Schizanthus**. They should be relatively easy to find at your local garden center. Trust me, the reason I put them in pots is because they put on a good show!

After years of growing and selling bedding plants, I've come to know the winners – **Madness petunias**, for example; people keep coming back for them year after year, and for good reason – they are simply the best petunia on the market.

**I do recommend hybrids for most varieties**, so read the tag when you shop. Look for F1. That symbol lets you know that the plants are first generation hybrids. You might pay a little more but you'll reap dividends.

What the heck's a hybrid you say? That's when plants are crossed to get the desired traits out of the seeds they produce. The new plants then will have the best qualities of the two parents. It might get disease resistance and vigor from one plant and earliness and hardiness from the other.

If you let your hybrid go to seed and then sow those seeds, the plants you get from that generation will be F2 and they will not be like the mother plant. The flowers may be smaller, the leaves bigger, the color lighter, the blossoms later. Let's just say that a hybrid is the qualities of two plants merged to create a better version than both parent plants, and that the seeds it produces are a weaker version of the original. Got that?

Some plants won't bloom if the days are too short, or if the days are too long. Fuschias, for example, won't bloom unless they've been exposed to 12 hours, or more, of daylength (daylight) for 25 days. Marigolds prefer fewer hours of light in order to bloom.

There are now varieties that are day neutral. In other words, they don't care as much about the amount of light they get, and will bloom on and on. So if a day neutral variety is available, in the color and height that you want, in whatever species you want, then buy that one over an ordinary variety.

You should also know that some species come in single varieties and in double versions. Double means that they have more than one row of petals. Wild roses are single. Roses from the florist are doubles.

Plant researchers and developers are always coming out with new varieties and colors. Don't be bashful. Experiment. Newer isn't always better but many times, with plants anyway, it's worth checking it out.

By the way, you might want to try out varieties that win the AAS award. That's the All American Selection award to you! These are plants that are planted in test plots everywhere in North America. In Canada alone there are 12 such plots from Vancouver, British Columbia to Edmonton and Calgary, Alberta to Borden and Winnipeg, Manitoba to York, Prince Edward Island.

In order to win, they have to do very well, pretty well everywhere! These plants are usually a good bet, even if they won the award 3 or 4 years ago.

Following is a list of some of the varieties I used in making up the pots for the recipes in this book. They are the ones I recommend. Mind you, I base my opinion on my experience, in my area; your area and experience might be different from mine. In that case, feel free to use your favorite varieties, or those available in your area. There are so many to choose from.

**I've only included the plants that I feel have an outstanding variety, or varieties, and those that need some explanation.**

AGERATUM: These fluffy little pompoms have been around for a long time and are very reliable. Remember, with this little guy blue is not blue; it is a shade of mauve or purple and can even be on the pinky side.

**ALYSSUM:** I love **Snow Crystals**. It's a white alyssum with bigger florets and is very vigorous. Although all alyssums are good, the **New Carpet of Snow** and **Navy Blue** don't bolt as quickly in extreme heat. If you're using two different colors of this plant in the same situation, they don't all have to come from the same series. It's true that **Wonderland White** and **Wonderland Rose** will come into bloom at about the same time, but that really doesn't make any difference to you unless you own a greenhouse and want to impress your customers with a show of color.

**ASTERS:** There's a great range of sizes here so make sure you get the variety that will give you the height you want. The shorter ones bloom sooner than the taller ones, but most varieties of asters are late bloomers that can put on a great show well into the end of the growing season. Try **Pot And Patio** – they're day neutral so they put on a show all summer.

**BEGONIAS:** Wow! What a show they put on – but beware – there are a whole slew of varieties here.

First, you have tuberous begonias – as the name implies, they come from bulbs. The **American Giants** have impressive 4 to 6" (10 to 15 cm) blossoms.

There are varieties that are started from seed and then develop into a bulb – the **Non-Stop**, the **Illumination**, **Pin Up**, etcetera. These have the same beautiful blossoms as the **American Giant**, only a smaller version on a smaller plant, and they bloom a little more profusely. I've called this type of tuberous begonia **Non-Stop** in the recipes, just to make life simpler.

Then, there are the fibrous begonias. They are different in that they have ordinary "fibrous" roots, rather than bulbs. The flowers are completely different, too – they're quite tiny but, of course, the plants are loaded with color! Keep in mind that not all varieties are the same height.

**CHRYSANTHEMUM:** There are some mums that have been developed for bedding plants. One such mum is **Snowland**. "But isn't it a daisy?" you say. Well, it looks exactly like a daisy, as do many chrysanthemums. **Yellow Buttons** is a yellow mum that goes by the latin name **Multicaule**.

**COSMOS:** Again, this is a plant that offers a lot of variety choices. **Sonata** blooms profusely on about 18" (45 cm) stems, short for this species.

**DIANTHUS:** There are great new varieties of an already great plant; The **Ideals, Floral Lace,** the **Parfait,** and now the **Diamond** series. Dianthus naturally prefer cooler weather, but they've been bred to tolerate a lot of heat and still produce an abundance of flowers.

**DIASCIA:** The varieties started from seed germinate like weeds and perform very well.

**GERANIUMS:** Here's a variety that needs some explanation. There are many different types.

SEED geraniums are just that – they're started from seed and are generally less expensive. That's why they were developed – to sell as bedding-out plants and in packs. Their blossoms are smaller than those of the zonals and the plants do not bush out as much.

ZONAL geraniums are usually double or semi-double geraniums started from cuttings or cloned. This means that they don't vary much from plant to plant and from generation to generation. The big advantage here is that the florets don't blow away at the first sign of a breeze! The flowers are bigger and the plants are tougher. Newer varieties of zonals are generally more disease resistant than the older ones. They are also more compact while still putting out outstanding flowers.

IVY geraniums were developed to trail and they have smooth shiny leaves as opposed to fuzzy leaves. The newer varieties have petals that kind of disappear into the foliage when the flower is done blooming, rather than falling off the plant and onto the ground or your patio floor.

**GRASSES:** In this part of the world many an hour is spent pulling out quackgrass, so why would anyone deliberately plant it in a pot? Because some of us like it, that's why. I've found that **Fountain Grass,** which I like and which is popular, can get too big for many pots. I decided to try **briza maxima** and liked it, so then I grew **briza minor.** You have to start these quite early if you don't plan on buying them at a greenhouse. I found the seeds at a local discount store so they're readily available.

**GYPSOPHILA (BABY'S BREATH):** In the last few years, new varieties have come out as bedding plants that will bloom all summer long, and are compact and short. They can also be trimmed to whatever height you want. Specifically, there are two, both of which won the AAS award in the year they were introduced: **Garden Bride** and **Gypsy.**

**LOBELIA:** Here's an old-fashioned flower that has made a comeback in a big way. What some people don't know is that it comes in a rainbow of colors and that it doesn't always trail; yes, there are upright types and they're really wonderful too. For trimming, see the TIP on page 71.

**MARIGOLDS:** If you like marigolds, boy are there ever a whole lot to like! They range from 8" (20 cm) to 3' (1 m) in height! The flower size ranges from tiny to huge. They come in all shades of yellow, gold and orange. Some are day neutral – mostly in the 12 to 16" (30 to 40 cm) range.

There are also marigolds that have single blossoms, and some that have double pompom-type flowers, not to mention the open-faced, flat-flowered plant. There's also the tiny-flowered, ferny-leafed type.

AFRICAN marigolds are the taller varieties – over 12" (30 cm). This is where you'll find day neutral types; and there are more and more coming out every year. Although there are many good varieties in this category, I especially like **Atlantis**. This is also where you'll find this year's new **Sweet Cream**, a creamy-white flower, which I've used in some of my recipes.

FRENCH marigolds are the short varieties with smaller flowers than the African. You don't see 3 to 4" (7 to10 cm) flowers on these guys. It's more in the 2 to 2½" (5 to 6 cm) range. This category is where the singles fit in, and the flat-faced ones, too. The color varies a lot more here, too, with red and yellow bi-colors and maroon and deep orange, and so on and so on. They grow anywhere from 8" (20 cm) to 12" (30 cm).

We're not done yet. There are the SIGNATA or SIGNET left. These are the fern-leafed marigolds that look airy and light. They grow 8 to 12" (20 to 25 cm) tall and have very small flowers. In this category, you'll find the **Gems** and **Lulu**. They're sometimes called rock garden marigolds because of the short bouquet they form.

There, now we're done with marigolds.

**NEMESIA:** These little sweethearts are making a comeback. First, **Sundrops** was introduced and then the **Nebula** and **Stargate** series, with **Stargate** coming in individual colors. **Sundrops** is an early variety and was in full bloom when I was making up my pots so I had the luxury of choosing my colors. Quite frankly, I was impressed by this plant's performance; it was blooming in early June and still going strong at first frost!

**PANSIES:** Here we go again! Too many to choose from!

Now, with pansies, there are the old-fashioned types, with faces or blotches; then there are the clear types that are all one color. All varieties are more or less the same height, but the flower size varies. Some, like **Bingo** and **Happy Face** have flowers that face up. **Dancer** is a great mix that blooms early. **Purple Rain** is a new variety that has a smaller flower on a plant that tends to cascade. There are also varieties that produce huge flowers – a full 4" (10 cm) across!

Add to this the new miniatures which are halfway between a viola and a pansy; **Baby Bingo** (which, by the way, really impressed me by its compact performance) and **Velour** are two varieties that I'm familiar with. These are really sweet and can take more heat and sun than the true pansies.

How to choose? First, decide if you want clear, blotched or a mixture of both, then, stick to hybrids. They're all generally good, and can usually take full sun, though I wouldn't suggest a hot spot for them.

**PETUNIAS:** Petunias are a bit like hamburger – you may not like it a whole lot but you can't ignore its versatility!

Petunias give you a wide color range, flower size range and now plant size range. They'll put up with frost and heat. They love to put on a show! They just cannot and will not be ignored!

Okay, here we go. GRANDIFLORA petunias have very large flowers, hence the grand in the grandiflora. The newer varieties stay quite compact all summer long. I like the **Dreams** series or the **Falcon**, and I'm sure the new kid on the block, the **Storm**, is also very good. The **Supercascade** series has very large flowers and the plant is more sprawling than compact. It has its place in hanging baskets and window boxes but is not the best in gardens.

The MULTIFLORA petunias are the old-fashioned type that have more but smaller blossoms – and an abundance of flowers. When these were improved, they became the new and improved FLORIBUNDA – a multitude of flowers on a much more compact plant. I'll say it again, you can't beat the **Madness** series in this category. As a matter of fact, that's all I use in the pots I make up, unless a customer specifically asks for something else. Not only are they tough and compact, they pop right up again after a rain – rather than looking like wet kleenex. If you're not sure what to use in these recipes, go **Madness** – you won't regret it.

MILLIFLORA petunias have not been out for very long; they're real sweethearts! They're new enough so that there is only one variety of its' type – the **Fantasies**. Even if you're not a fan of petunias, I think you would like these. The flowers are very small and dainty. The plants themselves stay 8 to 10" (20 to 25 cm) tall, and are compact.

As if all this weren't enough, there are also double-flowered petunias. These also come in GRANDIFLORA, FLORABUNDA, and MULTIFLORA. They, too, can be beautiful, looking like huge carnations. However, they haven't been developed as much as the single and don't bloom nearly as profusely. That's not to say that they don't have their place. Like the **Supercascade** single petunias, doubles have a tendency to sprawl and this is some people's cup of tea. Actually, the newer varieties like the **Cascade** series have a certain charm and look quite exotic in window boxes and in pots. They also bloom more than the older varieties. The **Double Madness** series performs very well, too, with more and smaller flowers on a compact plant. Now that the single petunias are so fully developed, I expect someone will take up the cause of doubles, and there should soon be newer and better performing varieties that can compete well with any other petunia.

Not only are there different sizes and colors of flowers, added to all that is different patterns of flowers. There are the **picotee**, which have a white edge on all the variously colored petunias. They look nice massed in landscaped gardens. The white is just enough to bring out the color of the petunias and brighten things up a bit. They are a series of their own, so there isn't a picotee Falcon or Madness. Mind you, there are some doubles with that feature and they are very striking; I'm thinking of the **Purple** or the **Rose Pirouettes**.

Then there are the stars, which are striped and so, yes, they look kind of star-shaped. Their effect is very much the same as the **picotee**. These are available in multiflora or grandiflora and are part of the **Madness** series or the **Ultra** or **Storm**.

When it comes to the height that petunias grow, don't believe everything you read. Some tags will say 10" (25 cm) high. Perhaps under the best of conditions, the petunias will stay that height, but normally they all grow to 12 or 14" (30-35 cm) except, of course, the **Fantasies**.

You should keep in mind that different colors sometimes behave differently. For instance, white usually grows taller than other colors, and so does carmine. Yellow is also more vigorous than purple or red.

Speaking of colors, I have yet to see a true blue petunia, yet there are still some series that insist on calling purple, blue. I have more respect for the newer varieties that call purple **Midnight** or **Royal** or some such thing. Now that you know that, when some recipe calls for purple petunias, don't go looking for a petunia that is actually called purple!

WAVE petunias are the rage these days. These come from seed and are single and cascade. When I say cascade, I mean cascade! They easily grow to at least 2' (60 cm) across. What you should know about this series is that not all colors are created equal. The purple (the original wave) hugs the ground, growing only about 4" (10 cm) high. The rose and pink have more of a tendency to mound but don't seem to get quite as wide. The lilac is very vigorous. There are new colors coming out but the purple still has a distinctive habit that is different from all the rest.

All colors of **Waves** grow so fast they need more fertilizer than other petunias. Other than that they are easy to grow and can handle a lot of stress.

To top this all off, there are also VEGETATIVE petunias. Like some types of geraniums, these are petunias that are reproduced by cuttings or clones and cannot be replicated by seed. In this category, you have the **Surfinias** and **Supertunias** and counting. You can bet on these to cascade and spread – a lot like the Wave series with different choices of colors. These are the most expensive of petunias, simply because they need to be fiddled with by the growers who then sell them to the greenhouses who then sell them to you! They need a bit more attention at home, too, than the regular petunias.

**SCHIZANTHUS:** Here's another old-fashioned flower I've been growing for years that's getting attention from seed developers. There's also an F1 hybrid available now. The varieties available in the past have performed just fine for me, so you can't really go wrong.

**SNAPDRAGONS:** One of my all-time favorites, this is another old-fashioned flower that has gone through all kinds of changes and been consistently popular. Besides the great variety of heights you can get, there's now the flower size difference.

This difference in flower size is not as dramatic as in petunias and pansies but, still, not all blossoms are created equal. We now have the azalea-type of blossom and the ordinary dragon's-mouth-type we all grew up with. This is not that big a deal, because the flower is composite and, because it's made up of a bunch of little florets, unless you're up close it's hard to tell which is which. One is as good as the other as far as performance and color are concerned.

The shorter types bloom earlier and stay in bloom longer than the taller types. Deadheading the shorter plants is not as important as it is with those 14" (35 cm) and over. Quite frankly, in these short varieties, I'm not sure which to recommend. Most are very good – the **Chimes**, the **Floral Carpet** and **Floral Showers** series, the **Bells,** the **Tahiti**, too. Those are all very short. A bit taller is the **Sweetheart** and a sweetheart it is! Then you get to the 12 to 18" (30 to 45 cm) **Sprites**, and to the taller, but still sturdy and proliferous bloomers, the new **Ribbons** and the **Labellas**. To tell the truth, I wouldn't go much taller than that in a pot. You just don't get the constant blooms with the giants.

**VIOLAS:** These little pixies must come from some fairyland. They are delicate and airy, yet bright and cheerful, with expressive little faces. They're also tough and can take heat and a great amount of cool. I especially like the **Princess** series, the **Velours**, and the **Sorbet**.

**ZINNIAS:** Again, there are all types of zinnias and, again, there's a formerly little-known zinnia making a come-back. This is the zinnia **Angustifolia**, also known as **Classic** zinnia, now available only in orange, and the new **Crystal White**. These zinnias are miniature and have a rather cascading habit.

Now you have an overview of the basics. If you feel you need more information, find more books, talk to your gardening friends, join your local horticultural society; above all give growing a chance. The best way to learn is to dive in, experiment, then find what suits you best. The laws of gardening are really minimal, the joys of gardening, bountiful. So get growing!

# BASIC
# KNOW-HOW

**Y**ou can read as many cookbooks as you like, but unless you get to it and do it, you'll never know the satisfaction of pleasing your own palate. Now that you know all that you need to know about ingredients for a delightful basket, success is within your reach. Begin as you would if you were whipping up a meal. Mix, sprinkle, pour, add, bake. Work from the ground up. Mix that soil, sprinkle in fertilizer, pour in some water, add baby plants and bake at medium heat all summer long!

## PLANT SELECTION:

When it comes to shopping for produce, I'm sure you take the time to check out the oranges, making sure they're firm, or that the apples aren't bruised; the lettuce isn't wilted. Shopping for plants demands the same vigilance.

Rule number one – read the tag to make sure you're getting what you want. Now check out the plant. Stay away from long, leggy specimens. If the leaves are yellowed or droopy, the plant could be diseased or infested with bugs.

Even if the plant is a healthy green, check out the underside of the leaves – you're looking for bugs. This is where aphids, spider mites and mealy bugs hang out. Look closely, because any bugs you can see easily are not very dangerous, it's the little wee guys you need to worry about.

Another spot insects like is the tender new growth and flower buds. Spider mites spin their fine webs there and this is where aphids feed.

Learn to be discriminating. It's fine to buy bargain plants, but remember that a cheap plant that dies on you is not much of a bargain. The price difference is not as important as the quality difference. Have the plants you were thinking of buying been mistreated? When shopping, notice if there are any drooping plants or plants that have leaves with dried up edges. These are signs of drought. They may be cheaper, but chances are they weren't looked after as well as they should have been. Bedding plants don't have large reserves of soil, so if they dry out it doesn't take long to dehydrate the roots. The plants will come back but, if dried out, they've been set back.

Look for short, bushy plants with dark green leaves. Take one out of its pot, if you can, and take a look at the roots. They should be white and well distributed. Is the soil somewhat moist? These are good signs. Or are the roots brownish, thick, and wound round and round. Can you see the soil, or is it solid roots? That's a sure sign the plant is much too root bound, and definitely not for you. After you've slipped the plant back into its container, try to look innocent . . . (Actually, any nursery worth its salt will be happy to provide this service for you so don't be afraid to ask.)

What size plants should you be buying? The small ones in the cell packs or the individual 4" (10 cm) pots? My experience has been that if you use younger plant material, the plants end up blending much more than when bigger plants are used. Mind you, if it's the end of June and you need a show for the middle of July, then go big. I guess it depends somewhat on when you want your containers at their prime, and also on your pocketbook. You will be paying more for the big guys. What is all-important here is that all plants be at about the same stage. If you have well-advanced petunias and little teeny marigolds in the same pot, chances are the petunias will end up taking over, simply because they will shade the poor little marigolds and suck up more water and nutrients.

Even here, there is always an option. I made up the Ambrosia recipe on page 101, with a rather advanced schizanthus and with big pansies. The lobelia was not very big at all. So I trimmed almost a third of the schizanthus and cut all the flowers and long stems off the pansies. That pot was gorgeous come the end of July, and it performed well right until freeze-up, and after!

## CONTAINERS:

Angel food pans – they're great – you don't even need to grease them! As a matter of fact, if you do, you'll ruin your cake! But if you forget to butter your pan when you're making brownies, you're in trouble . . . ! And pan size can make or break a naniamo bar recipe. In container gardening, container choice and preparation is important too.

As with anything else, check the label when you're buying a container; and bring a measuring tape along! Some labels will give you the outside measurement of a pot and others will give you the inside measurement, but no label will tell you which measurement it's using. So measure. You want the inside measurement. That means that the sign may say 16" (40 cm) pot, but the actual size is 12" (30 cm). Then you know why it's so cheap . . .

If your container has been used before, clean it with bleach and water. Make sure there are holes in the bottom. If your pot is wood or plastic, you can use an electric drill to make holes in it. Three or four ¼" (.5 cm) holes should do it.

Most plastic plant containers that you buy have little indentations where the holes should be. These can be poked out with a hammer and nail. If your plastic container has no indentations, don't try this; the plastic will likely crack – and there goes your pot! Using an electric drill works best, or try the following trick.

This tip is for the courageous person, owner of a plastic pot, ready to try anything! If you decide to go this route, keep your oven mitts handy. Heat up a nail on the element of your stove, pick it up with pliers and melt a hole into the bottom of your pot. It really works well, but you do need to be cautious.

Whichever way you do it, just make sure there are holes on the bottom of each and every container!

Wire pots, by the way, are a special case. They tend to drain wherever the plants are planted.

## FILLING:

If you make a cake from scratch but forget to put in baking powder, your cake will be a flop waiting to happen. The adding, stirring, combining and mixing – in other words, the putting it all together – this is the heart of planting.

You've decided what type of soil you're going to use . . . right? Now is the time to mix in the balanced 14-14-14 slow-release fertilizer. FOLLOW INSTRUCTIONS.

You can mix the soil and fertilizer in the pots you plan to use, or use a large container, mix first and then fill your pots. A child's plastic swimming pool works well, or a large plastic tub of any kind. It's fine to add some water at this stage, but just enough to settle the dust.

If you decide to put garden or topsoil in the bottom of your pot, don't worry about mixing fertilizer into it. Just throw it into the pot. NOW fill the container with the rest of the soil or soilless mix, making sure you have the slow-release fertilizer mixed into THAT part of it.

If your pot or pots are very large – a half-barrel or a 20" (50 cm) diameter container – you can cheat without your plants suffering. Fill your container about half full with peat moss, foam packing chips, even sawdust. Whatever you have around that is not too heavy and not toxic will do. Fill up the rest of your pot with your choice of soil.

When you make muffins or cupcakes, you fill the molds about ⅔ full. That's fine for muffins but it's a mistake for container gardening. Rather, fill your pot all the way up to the rim!

DO NOT PACK. Don't pack anything! Not the soil, the soil mix, the soilless mix. Pack nothing! What happens when soil is packed is that the water and the oxygen have no space in which to travel The top gets all bogged up and the bottom is still dry as a bone!

Take out the hose instead, or a watering can, and give your pots a good watering with a nice, soft flow. Let the pots sit and absorb that water. You want the pots to be moist all the way through. You will notice that the soil level has gone down somewhat. Now is the time to add more soil, if it's down more than an inch (2.5 cm) or so. Either way, water again and take it easy. This is like letting bread dough rise so . . . Have a cup of tea, go to work, play with the kids – whatever. Give the soil a chance to suck up the water in every crook and cranny!

Before you plant the pot, check the moisture one more time and water again if it isn't nice and moist all the way through.

## PLANTING:

Now that you've taken the time to plan what you want in your pots, come up with a color scheme, done your shopping, filled your container, you're getting down to the nitty gritty. And just like the real fun in baking a cake is playing with the icing and doing the decorating; the real fun in container gardening is planting time!

First thing – water the plants well. They'll be much easier to take out of their containers that way. You'll also be reducing transplanting shock by supplying the plants with water. Again, if you water early enough for the plants to absorb the water but not be soaking wet when you go to plant, you'll be ahead of the game. The roots will be damp, but not so wet as to be muddy and have all the soil drip away.

Because you don't want the root ball to dry out, don't take the plants out of their containers till you need them.

You know what a pain it can be to get a cake out of the pan without it breaking up; getting plants out of containers can be just as frustrating. I have some ideas to offer.

If your plants are in individual pots here's how you do it: slip your hand over the pot, with the plant fitting between your index and middle or ring finger. Now turn the pot upside down. Give the bottom of the pot a firm tap with your trowel. If the plant does not slip out, tap the sides of the pot and give the bottom another (gentle) whack. The plant should now be bundled in your hand. Put the pot down. Gently turn your plant right side up and set it in the hole.

It's a good idea to do this over the filled container; not only does it make less mess, but you can get to the hole you've dug that much faster if the root ball is falling apart!

Getting plants out of an open pack is very much the same – but easier. Actually an open pack (that's a container that's not divided into individual cells) is the easiest to get plants out of. Once you've got the plants out, just cut it up evenly, as you would a cake.

Cell packs are another story. If there's a hole in the bottom of each cell, it's easy. Stick the blunt end of a pen or pencil in the hole and push up. DO NOT PULL THE PLANT OUT. That's the best way to lose your baby! If there are no holes in the cell pack, try this: pinch the bottom and the plant should pop up. Or, with your fingers on the top rim, push up on the bottom of the cell with your thumb. If the plant does not pop out, pinch the sides of cells a bit. Now, try the thumb trick again. If all else fails, and you're boiling over, cut or rip the darn thing apart!

All right, you've got your main plant out – your focus plant – the one that goes in the middle. That's where you start. The middle.

With a trowel, or with your hands, dig a hole the same depth, or slightly deeper, than the root ball that goes into it. If the root ball is quite tight – root bound – loosen the soil on the root ball by scratching all around it. Put your plant in the hole and push the excess soil back over the roots and around the stem. Tuck the plant in gently, all around. It's important for the plant to be firm in the soil, but it's also important to not pack the soil too much.

Now place the next row of plants. Take Burgundy Drama on page 84 as an example. There's a yellow petunia in the middle. Set three burgundy petunias around the yellow one; lay them on top and position them in a triangle. Use a trowel to push the soil aside and transplant the three petunias.

When there is no centerpiece, as in Salmon Simplicity on page 73, find the center and put in a stick or marker and work around it.

I used to try to get most of the edge plants as close to the rim as possible, but after hearing two different experts (one of them being Lois Hole) say that it's better to keep them away from the edge, I keep these plants a good 2" (5 cm) away from the side and put them in at a slant. When you slant a plant in, not only are the roots not so close to the side of the pot, where they may dry out faster, the plant is also encouraged to cascade a little more. When you plant this way, you have to watch more carefully that you've covered every root hair. Exposed roots do not contribute to the health of the plant.

Once you're done, water the plants in evenly, with a gentle, flowing shower. This also cleans plants and containers of soil and mucky finger prints.

A coco- or moss-lined container has its own set of rules, if you decide to put plants around the sides of it. It isn't necessary to put plants on the sides if you'd rather not or if you like the look of the moss or coco liner – just remember to arrange for drainage. One reason these containers are popular is the earthy, natural look of the moss or coco; the other is that when they're fully planted they look like a whole ball of flowers with plants coming out in every direction! That's where the name color ball comes from.

Apparently the coco or the moss is supposed to help retain moisture, and insulate the roots from heat. Now, this is true in some climates, but certainly not everywhere. In a dry, windy climate as in western Canada, the wind blows through the liner in a hurry and constant watering becomes a way of life. So it's common to use a plastic liner inside the coco or moss. This helps the moisture problem and still allows the coco and moss to insulate.

By the way, you can cheat with a wire basket and not use either a moss or coco liner. Give jute a try. It worked well when I tried it, and I've also seen large wire pots lined with jute. They were quite high up and had no plants in the sides, so the jute was very evident – and it looked good. It doesn't have the insulating property of the other liners but it's easy to work with.

To fill a moss- or coco-lined pot or basket, you actually layer the soil; that means emptying the pot of that lovely moist soil you put in and prepared so meticulously. If you're using a coco liner, wet it by dipping it in a pail of water, or by hosing it down. This makes it easier to handle. Now, if you live in an area where the air is dry, line the inside of the liner with a plastic garbage bag and trim the edges. You can leave it double if you like.

You have an option here; if your pot is small or if watering is a concern, add a saucer before filling in with soil. This can be a pot saucer or an aluminum pie plate – anything that will hold a bit of water. The water will collect in the saucer and be available for the plants' roots when they need it.

1 & 10 *Ring of Fire, 12" & 14", page 83*
2       *Plum Pudding, page 77*
3       *Partly Pink, page 80*
4       *Élégance, page 71*
5       *Peach Custard, page 80*
6       *Summer Extravagance, page 132*
7       *Burgundy Drama, page 84*
8       *Pretty in Pink, page 72*
9       *Éclair, page 122*

Then comes the tricky part; planting the darn thing! Put in a layer of soil 2 to 3" (5 to 8 cm) deep, depending on the depth of the basket. With a sharp kitchen or utility knife, poke a hole through the liner or moss and the plastic. Keep slicing upwards and then across, so that you end up with a cut in the form of an X.

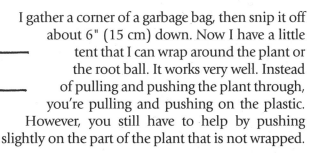

Now put in a plant. That's easier said than done too; it's important not to break off the roots and not to damage to the stems and leaves. One way you can do this is to wrap a piece of plastic around one end of the plant; stick that part of the plant through the hole and then pull out the plastic.

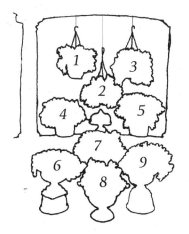

I gather a corner of a garbage bag, then snip it off about 6" (15 cm) down. Now I have a little tent that I can wrap around the plant or the root ball. It works very well. Instead of pulling and pushing the plant through, you're pulling and pushing on the plastic. However, you still have to help by pushing slightly on the part of the plant that is not wrapped.

Do you put the plant in from the inside and put the leaves through the hole, or do you stick the root end in from the out-side? Good question. The answer depends a lot on the size of the plant, the size of the root ball and the type of plant.

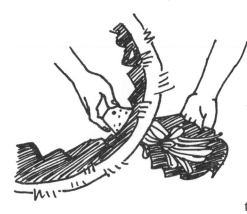

If you're dealing with a begonia or impatiens, or any other plant that has watery stems, stick the roots in the opening. But if you have a petunia or a lobelia plant, which has more flexible stems and leaves, then put the leaves through the hole, toward the outside.

Now that you have positioned the plants that you plan on using around the bottom end of the pot, put in another layer of soil and, believe it or not, firm it a bit, especially around the root ball. The problem is that if the roots can get into the hole, they can fall out, too!

Next step – start all over again! Keep going till you're all out of plants. Once the edges are done, it's time to do the top. This part is easy to do; you just follow the instructions for a regular pot.

Whatever kind of pots you have, when you've finished filling and watering, leave them in a sheltered spot, against the house (in the shade), under a tree canopy or in your garage. Leave your pot or pots there until they settle in – a day or overnight. If the plants have just come from the greenhouse, toughen them up by leaving them in a sheltered spot and covering them with a blanket, a sheet, a towel, or sheets of newspaper in the evening and uncovering them in the morning. Do this for three or four nights, then set them where you want them. By the way, this is called **"hardening off"** or "acclimatizing" your plants.

**If you're filling your pots early in the season, watch out for frost and always have that blanket ready! Notice I say blanket, sheet, towel or paper and not plastic. Cloth, even paper, does a better job of protecting plants than plastic does. A light sheet often works better than a heavier plastic.**

As far as timing goes, I can't tell you exactly when to plant your pots. Summer's short, it's true, so you may be tempted to plant early. That isn't a problem as long as you protect them from frost, but if you want your plants to be at their best later in the season, for a wedding or other social occasion or simply because that's what you want, then hold off on planting.

For customers that like to have color in June, I start the pots in early to mid May, right around Mother's Day. For those that prefer the show to be at its best in mid to late August, I start in the middle of June. I recommend that you not plant pots past the 20 or 21 of June. By the time they hit their prime, fall will have set in firmly.

## WATERING:

Following recipes is great. A cup of this, a teaspoon of that – it's easy. Then, there are those dishes that are a little harder to define. Like gravy. Do you add potato water? What about carrot water? How much do you put in? Exactly how much flour do you put in to get the consistency that you want. You have to go by guess and by golly until you've got enough experience to know what you are doing. Making good gravy is somewhat of an art. So is watering.

Watering is also very important. Think about it; plants dry out – they wilt; plants get bogged down with too much water – they wilt. Bring out the artist in you; take out the hose!

It's important to water your plants right through. Let the water drain out the bottom. This will help flush out any unwanted build-up of salts and minerals. If your plant starts to droop – water immediately. It will not die. Mind you, it's a good idea to keep up with your watering so that the poor plants don't feel the need to spell out that they're thirsty by passing out! Near death experiences are certainly something they prefer to avoid.

By the way, the best way to kill a plant is to overwater it. If your plants are wilted but the soil is moist, it could be that the plants are telling you that they need to dry out a bit.

Yes, watering is a fine art, but anyone can learn enough technique to keep plants beautiful.

Watering in the morning is the very best. Watering in the hottest part of the day is not a great idea, but anytime is better than not at all; just make sure you fit it into your schedule. You'll want to water every day in hot dry weather, but ease off on cooler days. As the plants mature, so will the roots, and they'll slurp that water up a lot quicker than when they were babies. Keep that in mind. Also, keep in mind that bigger pots may not need water every day, and that small ones may need to be watered in the morning AND in the afternoon.

When a cake has pulled away from the sides of the pan, it's a good indication that it's cooked. If the soil pulls away from the sides of the pot, it's a good indication it's cooked, too. So water before that happens. Check the moisture by sticking a finger into the soil. It may look dry on the surface and still be quite moist underneath. Wait until the top ½" (1.25 cm) or so is dry before you water again . . . and remember, water well. At least once a week, water enough for the water to drain right through.

A good thing to remember, too, is to water over the entire surface of the pot – not just the middle or one side. The water will drain down, but it isn't likely to travel across, so wave that wand!

As for your moss- and coco-lined pots, make sure you water till the water starts coming out of the bottom as well as the spots where there are flowers planted in on the sides. It's a little tricky to do but it is very important. What I've found is that if any plants keel over, it's more likely to be the ones near the bottom; when I've checked them out by sticking a finger near their roots, I've found them to be dry. Another thing you can do to help the guys on the bottom is to make sure you give them a shower when you water. The leaves will absorb the humidity, so it should help them a bit – you need to give them all the assistance you can.

For any pot, it's good to water, then let the pot sit for a while, then water again; that way you avoid over-watering and still water until the water drains through. If you have quite a few pots, start at one end, water each pot – then start over again at pot numero uno.

Get rough with your plants once in a while. Using cold water, turn your nozzle to a good brisk spray, then shoot your plants. You can even try to get to the underside of the leaves by turning your nozzle upside down underneath them. Bugs really hate that . . . Spidermites, aphids and other insects fall off, fly off or drown. That's why you do it. As a matter of fact, this works as well as any insecticide to keep pesty populations under control.

By the end of the summer, you'll have had enough practice to be a fine water artist . . . or very good at doing the rain dance!

## FERTILIZING:

You know how teenagers are – no matter how much food you buy or prepare, it doesn't take long before they've eaten you out of house and home. Plants need nutrition, too, and there's not a whole lot of soil in a pot. And unlike teens, who can dig deep into their (or your) pocket for dough and then run to a fast food joint for lunch, **roots can't dig deeper when they run out of food! That's why it's important to feed your plants**.

Fertilizer is a bit like baking powder. A teaspoon (5 mL) of it will make things grow and look nice, a tablespoon (15 mL) can ruin things. What may happen if you over-feed your plants is that they will look lush and green and tall and bold, but will not bloom! They're so comfortable, they think they'll live forever and lose the need to reproduce. So whatever you do, **follow the instructions on the package**, and don't get carried away!

Use the type of fertilizer that fits in best with your lifestyle. If you are a bit of a procrastinator, you can think about what you want to do for a month to six weeks after transplanting. If you're a doer rather than a thinker, you can start your regime about two weeks after transplanting.

Don't worry about the brand of fertilizer you use; just check the label and make sure you have a complete fertilizer, then follow instructions.

If you decide to use a low-concentration fertilizer (that's the one with low numbers) you'll find yourself fertilizing more often. The plants actually rather like that because then they get a steady flow of nutrients. That's not to say that you should feel bad about using a high-concentration feed; plants are quite accommodating.

Should you decide to go with a higher-concentration fertilizer such as 20-20-20, you can really get lazy and fertilize only every couple of weeks, or even stretch it out to a month, depending on your soil, container size, number of plants and, of course, the weather.

Another alternative is to use the 20-20-20 but mix in TWICE the amount of WATER. Then you can use it more often if you like – every ten days or so.

You can water down your concentration, so why not just double up – use twice the amount of feed in the same amount of water called for in the instructions? The answer is simple – your plants will suffer from acute indigestion! They'll turn brown, shrivel up and possibly die.

If you aren't big on fertilizing, but notice midway along the season that the impatiens leaves are quite a pale green, or the salvia and petunia leaves are rather more of a lime green than a dark forest green, its time to get to it. The plants are carrying a sign that says "Feed me". Full strength 20-20-20 is the answer there.

There is one more specialty fertilizer you should know about. It's a type that's seen on a lot of garden center shelves and may be one that you've read about or tried. I'm talking about a **high phosphorous fertilizer**, a 10-52-10 or 10-60-10.

In container gardening, this type of fertilizer is only used once – when you transplant. It helps the roots get established and stays in the soil for a long time. If you decide to use it, do so once a season, then don't use it again.

I use this particular fertilizer when I'm in a mood where I feel the need to be a perfectionist; or when I start to doubt my growing abilities. It makes me feel better. How much of a difference it makes, I'm not sure. It's like adding sugar, or not, to the waffle dough; you're hard pressed to tell what difference it makes. Use 10-52-10 if you like, but don't feel you absolutely have to have it. Your plants will love you either way!

## LIGHT REQUIREMENTS:

Many old wood cookstoves had a temperature gage, but most of them did not have degrees indicated on them. Instead they had what old-fashioned recipe books called for: low, medium or moderate, and high. Since you have to go by feel for temperature and light, I've used the old way of doing things in my recipes.

I've called for sun, part sun; moderate heat – or for sun, part sun, high heat. In other words, I've tried to indicate not only the amount of light a plant needs, but also how much heat it will tolerate. **High heat** means you can go for the hot spots, **moderate** means out in the yard or on the east side, and **low** means in the shade. For example, if the recipe states part sun, sun; moderate to high heat, your pot can go in direct sun and in a hot spot. If it says part sun, sun; low to moderate heat, then put your container in direct sun or on the east side where it won't get too warm; reconsider putting it on the south side of a white house. If the instructions say shade, part sun; low to moderate heat, then stick the pot on the east side or in the shade. You're in luck if it says shade, part sun, sun; low to high heat. That means you can put that container where you darn well feel like it and it will do well.

I hope this will give you a better idea of where to place your pots; however, these pot recipes are not set in stone, so be flexible, try different locations and see for yourself.

I say this from experience. When I first started getting interested in plants, I bought godetia, read up on it, found out that it prefers shade, then proceeded to transplant it right up against the south side of my brown house. It thrived and, to boot, it came back the next spring!

## GENERAL CARE:

Have you noticed how some cooks have a real instinct for taste? They'll smell the soup, and from this hint, add a bit of salt, maybe oregano or a bay leaf. Maybe the soup already tastes great, but they'll add a pinch of this or that and really enhance it! Some gardeners have that ability. The rest of us need to learn. That's the good news – we can all learn.

You've stuck your finger in the soil, decided to water, or not; determined to fertilize, or not. Now what? Can your instinct cut in so that you pinch a bit of this or a bit of that and make that pot truly outstanding? You bet it can.

I learned my way to a green thumb from my mother-in-law, and her motto is **"you can't water without a pair of scissors"**! And it's true. Always carry scissors in your pocket when you water. That's when you're most likely to notice what needs to be done. The main thing is to **deadhead**. That means removing not only the faded flower but also the seed pod it has formed. That's why it's best to use scissors. If you pull off the petals, you're leaving the pod behind, and not doing that much good. Of course there's also the possibility that not only are you pulling off the petals, but the whole stem – or even uprooting the whole plant!

To me, the difference between deadheading and trimming is that **when you're deadheading you are removing faded flowers**, but **when you're trimming you're removing a whole stem or a portion of the plant**. When you trim, you may want (or not) to keep the shape of the plant. Take schizanthus as an example; it grows in the shape of a ball, so it's important to follow the shape as you cut. By the same token, you may trim a plant because you want to change its shape. If your petunias are getting leggy – cut them down. When I was busy testing out the recipes I used in this book, I found myself trimming the Purple Rain pansy quite a bit, just to give the geranium it was with a chance to grow, or even, at times, to make its companions visible to the naked eye.

There's quite a bit you can do if you want your pots to keep on blooming. You can deadhead your plants; trim off any brown leaves; weed if necessary; cut off ANY dead leaves or branches. Most of all, do not live in denial! Cut off, pull out, move out! If you notice that your plant is beginning to stretch up (get leggy), cut it or move it. If it droops every day at noon, even if it's well watered, maybe it's over-cooking; so move it. If it's looking straggly, cut it off. If it's completely dead, cut it out. That's what I said, cut it out! Be ruthless.

If you don't like it, if it's diseased, if it's leggy, pull it out. The other plants will fill in the empty space in no time! The remaining plants' roots will love the room and the extra nutrients. When it comes to plants, it's every plant for itself and may the best one bloom!

**The best way to learn is by doing. Watching someone mix pastry is a help, but getting down and dirty is a better learning experience.**

A plant's prime objective is to live, reproduce and die. It won't thrive under all conditions, but its will to live is strong, so as long as it has the basics it will live and bloom quite happily. Go ahead, give it your best shot and apply the KISS concept – **Keep It Simple, Sweetheart!**

# COOKING
# SECRETS

**P**resentation is everything! Jell-o in a mixing bowl is Jell-o. Jell-o set in a ring mold, unmolded onto a plate and garnished, is a festive dessert.

The same is true of container gardening. You don't have to have exotic plants to make a beautiful pot. It's all in the color combinations and plant arrangements.

This book is full of recipes, but we both know that ideas spawn more ideas that spawn more ideas and so on. Sometime along the way, you may want to design your own pot. When you make up a pot, you're actually arranging flowers – you become a fledgling florist, so you might as well learn a few basic elements of design.

## FOCUS:

A centerpiece dresses up any table. It can be a large bouquet of flowers or something as simple as a single candle. It draws the eye to it just because it's smack dab in the middle. It's the focus of your table.

In a container, the plant that sticks out the most is your focus plant; it's usually the biggest plant and it's usually in the middle of the pot. Just like the single candle, it doesn't have to be huge or even a lot bigger than the rest of the plants. Sometimes, just the fact that a plant blooms more than the rest makes it a focus plant. In other words, the focus plant is the plant that is the center of attention. This could be a petunia, a geranium, a begonia, a dracaena spike, or even a clump of grass (of course, in that case, we'd give it a fancy name – like briza maxima!).

Sometimes the focal point is the same as the line and fill. Some pots may not have a center plant but rather three plants that perform all three functions. The recipe Muffin Head on page 127 is a good example of that. The three petunias are the jacks-of-all-trades in this case.

In my mind it's important to have the focus in the center. Even though the pot may end up against a wall and will only be seen from one angle, it will be more balanced if you plant it from the center out. The advantage to this is that you can turn your pot to show off the best angle, and it will look better up close, too.

## LINE:

Because we don't want your eye to get stuck on one plant, we add line. This is what gives dimension to a pot. This is especially true in a hanging basket; you may want to put in vinca vine or English ivy, lobelia, morning glory, maybe thunbergia – anything that trails or cascades over the edge. Anything that adds height also gives line – in a patio pot a dracaena spike or another taller plant does that. You don't need a whole lot of it. A single plant will give your eye the hint to travel. Remember, too, that even though a dracaena spike works well to add line to a patio pot, it doesn't do much for a hanging pot, unless that pot is very large.

## MASS:

This is the main ingredient – like romaine lettuce in the Caesar salad. Two plants in a basket can work if they are a fuchsia and an English ivy, what with the fuschia bushing out and the ivy dripping over; but a statice with a vinca vine wouldn't impress anyone. Beautiful as statice can be, its flowers sit near the top of the plant and the stems and leaves are rather bare; the vinca vine, though it bushes out, does not spread around. You'd need mass to take up the slack. In the case of the fuchsia and the ivy, the fuchsia is both the focus and the mass. In the other case you would need to add another main color and texture. This might be a couple of petunias or marigolds, geraniums or pansies; or foliage plants like coleus, dusty miller or silver brocade artemesia.

## FILL:

Now that you have the focus plant and the mass, you need something to fill up all the nooks and crannys and to spill over the edge. This is fill. Fill makes a beautiful pot outstanding by adding interest and detail. It's the finishing touch, like the parsley on the plate!

## COLOR:

Getting back to salad, any salad, it's nice to add tomatoes or peppers or radishes. Something that will add color and when it comes to color, Mother Nature apparently has no taste. When I was little, there was a saying that, "Blue and green should never be seen". Everyone applied this rule with vigor. Yet the sky has always been various shades of blue, and trees have always been myriad shades of green. Take Mother Nature's example and put together the colors that you like.

If you love flowers, but feel unsure of color combinations, use a color wheel to guide you. You can put analagous colors together – orange, apricot, yellow, – or complementary together – orange and blue or yellows and purples. Analagous colors are side by side on the color wheel and give a softer more harmonious effect. Complementary colors are opposites and they add sizzle, high impact and drama to your pots. Hot pink, or rose, goes well with yellow, white, cream, blue or purple; and with other shades of pink. Red looks great with those colors too but clashes with deep pink. A soft pink is pretty with white, cream, blue or purple, but yellow doesn't do anything for it. Of course, any green variation will go with any color.

Sometimes, just a touch of one color will brighten up a whole pot. This is especially true of yellow and white. Darker colors will stand out and just a touch may be all you need. At other times, you may want to add foliage, cream or white to soften a combination.

There's nothing wrong with using one color, or one variety of plants. A pot of bright red petunias can be as striking against a white house as would a pot of mixed colors.

## TASTE:

Some people love peanut butter and onion sandwiches. It isn't my cup of tea, but what the heck, I'm not the one eating it. On the other hand, I like cooked, cooled lentils, mixed with mayonnaise, in my sandwich and, I can tell you, my husband and my kids certainly do not.

There is no accounting for taste and gardening is one of those rare areas where what you like is what you get, and if the next guy doesn't appreciate it, that's fine. I'm not fussy about marigolds or salvia or dusty miller in a hanging pot but some people like them very much. The area of taste is total anarchy – what anybody else thinks has nothing to do with what kind of arrangement you make. Remember that the next time you've put together a pot you're really proud of. Then, if your snooty neighbor or smart-alecky kid comes along saying, "My, my, that's . . . how should I put it . . . an interesting pot you've put together." or some even less complimentary remark, pay no attention. Gardening is a very personal relationship between you and nature, so forget the neighbor, forget your family, forget everything – enjoy what you like.

# MORE DIMES THAN DOLLARS

**C**ross rib roast is cheaper than tenderloin, and blade roast is an even cheaper cut. What you buy is a choice you make according to your budget. When container gardening you have a lot of choices along the way and, as in grocery shopping, you can cut corners. I have a few ideas and you know what ideas are like . . . they mushroom!

## CONTAINERS:

You can fake it and bake pizza in a frying pan or fry onions in a saucepan but, generally speaking, that kind of substitution is hard to do in the kitchen. A layer cake in a pizza pan just doesn't cut it. Not so with container gardening.

Plastic bags and containers, ice-cream pails, old pots, straw baskets, wooden crates, boots, washing machine or dryer drums, all are containers you can use. **Just remember to poke holes in the bottom!** I've seen a planter tree made up of ice-cream pails filled with Wave petunias! Once the petunias bloom and cascade, they hide the pots and the platforms they sit on.

Work or rubber boots work well if they're large enough. They certainly add interest to any patio or flower garden! Again, life will be easier if they're a large size and, yes, find a way to make holes in the bottom!

Businesses involved in appliance repairs are a good place to go for washing machine or dryer drums. These can stay "au naturel" or be painted.

| | |
|---|---|
| 1 | *Salmon Simplicity, page 73* |
| 2 & 10 | *Apricot & Peach Salad,* |
| | *10" & 12", page 78* |
| 3 | *Dainty Treat, page 75* |
| 4 | *Caribbean Lace, page 72* |
| 5 | *Piquante Daisy, page 126* |
| 6 | *Muffin Head, page 127* |
| 7 | *Summer Riches, page 128* |
| 8 | *Strawberry Sunday, page 89* |
| 9 | *Peach Punch, page 79* |

You may have seen the plastic bags that you can hang up on a wall or a fence, with holes cut out for transplants. The next time you buy shoes, keep the bag and give it a try. Once the plants have grown, you can't see the bag. Actually, the flower pouches sold in garden centers are not expensive to begin with and can be used for more than one season. Still, this is a good way to recycle, even if the money you save is negligible.

Baskets work very well. Straw laundry baskets are not expensive and make nice large pots. Garage sales abound with baskets, so keep an eye out for larger-sized ones. The trick here is to line them with plastic, cut holes in the bottom of the plastic, then fill.

Fiber pots are a good buy. Again, these are very earthy-looking and the sizes and shapes are very interesting. They are good quality at a decent price and can be reused for quite a number of years. Even the huge barrel-sized fiber pots are very reasonably priced.

As for wire baskets, they usually are a bit more money than the plastic, but they last forever. And quite frankly they don't really need the coco liner or the moss (see notes on page 32). As a matter of fact, the company that supplied me with wire pots sells them with the plastic liner included. Coco liners being what they are – quite a bit of work, and with being busy in the greenhouse as well as the test kitchen, I didn't use one in a lot of the pots I made up. The results were just fine.

Of course coco liners can be used more than one season so, if you buy one, save it from one season to the other. Reusing and recycling saves some cash.

Where I live, moss is easy to get at, we have lots of forests. If you live near trees, you can get out and gather moss. If you don't have moss readily available, you have to buy it from a nursery or garden supply shop.

January and February may seem like an unusual time to be buying containers, but some discount stores have very good deals on plastic pots and urns at that time. So check your flyers year round. Don't hesitate to buy used pots at garage sales and at junk dealers; check at your local greenhouse to see if they sell used pots.

1   *Sunny Boy, page 107*
2   *Fresh Mélange, page 95*
3   *Dew Drops, page 76*
4   *Chiffon Ruffle, page 141*
5   *Easter Egg Special, page 74*
6   *Butter Tart, page 102*
7   *Heaven Scent, page 133*

Keep in mind that there are times when it's best to spend a little more initially and have something really durable to last a lifetime. You could set yourself a goal of buying one or two pots a year till you have all you need.

One suggestion is pots made of polyethylene. These are absolutely beautiful pots, available in all shapes and sizes, that can face the elements and last forever without cracking or breaking.

In the same vein, terra cotta pots can last a long time if you look after them, and they can be quite reasonably priced. Again, if you decide to go the more expensive but last-forever-path, check out terra cotta that has been fired at more than 1000 degrees. These can be ignored through all the seasons and still come out in one piece – yes even the spring thawing and freezing and thawing cycle, and the way below zero temperatures of the north country!

Remember, any pot will last a lot longer if it is not left out in the elements for the winter. Empty your pots and store them in a garage, shed or basement.

## WATER:

To save water, try using drought resistant plants. Geraniums, petunias, portulaca and zinnias are just a few of the many varieties that need less water.

A good idea is to reduce the number of plants per pot; then the roots don't compete as much; the individual plants grow larger and still do the job, without nagging you all the time for a drink.

Yes, you can mulch pots with peat moss or compost to reduce the need to water; or insulate your pots. Use layers of newspaper as a liner for all of your pots.

If you have a lot of pots, using drip hoses will save you time and water.

**The most important thing is to remember the rules of watering: morning is best; water well and let the top dry out before you water again. Water not only your plants; get in there and water the soil as well.**

## PLANT MATERIAL:

There are many ways to save on groceries. One is to plant a garden but not necessarily a MARKET garden! Before you decide to start your own greenhouse, consider other options . . . when it comes to plant material . . . my, my . . . where to start. There are lots of ways to pinch pennies here, without starting a mammoth project. The best place to start is with other people's gardens! And the best place to have access to other people's gardens is through a horticultural society; so join the horticultural society in your town or city. You don't have to be an expert gardener to join. This is a great place for any gardener to be, from the beginner to the most experienced. The club members have a wealth of knowledge and are eager to share. Plant and seed exchanges are popular; there are talks by local gardeners and by experts; workshops and other activities ensure good value for the few dollars you spend to join. It's also a good place to team up with other people to buy, and share, plants.

"May I borrow a cup of sugar please . . . and half a hosta?" Get to know your neighbors! Sample their perennials! They do need to be divided every once in a while; many different varieties can be used in pots – lamium and arteme-sia are two that come immediately to mind.

Farmers' markets can also be a good place to buy plants. Of course, no matter where you obtain plants, be sure to inspect them for signs of pests and diseases before you take them home. Remember, bugs that are easy to see are usually harmless. It's those pesky aphids and spidermites you don't want to invite to your house.

House plants can do the trick, too. German ivy, English ivy, asparagus fern, rat-tail cactus – almost any trailing plant that is not too sensitive can be rooted and used as a pot accent. This is where green thumb neighbors come in handy; if you don't have houseplants, get to know someone who does!

Calculate and substitute. Sit down and figure out generally what you want, then substitute colors or omit varieties that might add to the pot but are not major ingredients. Check the prices on different varieties, too. One geranium may cost more than a half-dozen petunias or dianthus. In that case, if you're budgeting carefully, you'll want to do up pots that avoid geraniums. Of course that brings us to another point: overwintering.

Begonia bulbs, dahlia bulbs and geraniums can be an investment if you over-winter them in your cold room. If you only have a few bulbs, and you have the room, they'll keep well in your refrigerator. Begonias can be pulled out after the very first frost, dried, then kept in a paper bag. They need to be repot-ted in late winter or early spring. Dahlia bulbs may be kept with the soil intact. Take the whole thing, pot and all, and put it in your cold room.

Having to find ways to save money can sometimes force you to do things you may not otherwise try. Try starting some of your own plants from seed. There are people at horticultural meetings whose brains you can pick for information and know-how. Visit the library and get gardening books and magazines. Some seed catalogues include tips on seeding times and germination. Stokes Seed Catalogue was my growing bible when I started out.

If you decide to go this route, start small. It can end up being a bigger job than you think. Take into consideration the price of seed, soil, the room you'll need and the light requirements the plants need. In other words, do your homework. You'll be more likely to succeed and enjoy the job if you have an idea of what you're doing and what costs are involved.

There are some plant varieties you can seed directly into a pot. **Nasturtiums**, **alyssum**, **cosmos** and **zinnias** are a just a few examples. Put in more seeds than the number of plants you need, then pull out all but the most vigorous.

If you can't find the pennies to flower garden the way you'd like, or if you don't have the time, or won't be home most of the summer, encourage your neighbors. Then place your lawn chair in a strategic spot and enjoy the flowers of their labors. Just as wonderful kitchen odors can't be contained, a lovely view belongs to all who can see it!

Making jams and jellies, canning tomato sauce, pickles and relish, freezing peas and corn; what are we really trying to do here? We're trying to bring nature's bounty into our homes so that we can enjoy it all winter long. That's why refrigerators were invented – to conserve. We often try do the same with our summer crop of plants and flowers.

## QUALITY CONTROL:

You know the old adage: when in doubt, throw it out. The same is true of container gardening. If your main dish becomes infected with bugs, you'll end up having to throw it out. **Pest prevention is the key**. The chapter Basic Know-How on page 25, gives tips on pest and disease prevention by using common sense in the plant selection, watering and general care of your plants. However, if you do end up with a bigger population of bugs than what is generally considered healthy, I have a little recipe you can try.

I've used this in the greenhouse on spider mites, aphids and even thrips. Mind you, what I like to do in the greenhouse is to mix a bucketful and actually dip the plants in – head first, so to speak. I use the weaker concentration for snapdragons, chrysanthemums, begonias and peppers, but go whole-hog for geraniums, dracaena spikes, impatiens and most other plants.

I shared this secret recipe with the horticultural club at one of our meetings in Prince Albert. At a later session, we were talking about some destructive pests in delphiniums when one woman piped up that she had used this recipe and gotten rid of her's. Only – she forgot to dilute it! Apparently it had worked very well and even the delphiniums survived!. It's not something I would try and I certainly don't advise you to try it either. **Do dilute the concentrate!**

## Pest Prevention Concentrate

   **1 cup (250 mL) of liquid dishwashing soap**
   **(I recommend Sunlight)**
   **1 tablespoon (15 mL) of vegetable oil**

**Combine these 2 ingredients in a small container and stir well.**

# Pest Prevention Spray

**1 to 2 teaspoons (5-10 mL) of the concentrate on page 58**
**1 quart (1 L) of water**

Mix the 2 ingredients in a spray bottle and spray your plants with it, trying to get to the underside of the leaves as much as possible, and also flower buds and new shoots – anywhere bugs are likely to be. In very hot weather, repeat every third day (do 3 applications over 7 days) in warm to cool weather, repeat every week for 3 weeks (do 3 applications over 3 weeks).

If you have to, use pesticides, but please, do not use just any old house and garden spray. Remember that any bug killer is an insecticide for very specific bugs. If it's meant to kill mosquitoes or flies flying around in the air, that's what it should be used for. These aren't meant to spray directly on plants. I've heard many people say that they've used these sprays on all kinds of bugs on all kinds of plants. Some of the stories were sad – the bug lived, but the plant died. They really aren't meant to be used on plants, and can seriously harm the host more than the pest that lives on it. Rather than use the wrong pesticide, go to a nursery or garden center with enough of the infested plant material to let the person helping you figure out what the problem is. Then let that person recommend a product. All pesticides are not created equal.

When you get home, read the instructions BEFORE you use the product, then FOLLOW those instructions! And all will go well.

## OVERWINTERING:

Potatoes and carrots keep very well in a cold room and can be consumed all winter long. You can't actually enjoy your planted containers all winter long, but you can conserve them for next year. The recipe Summer Extravagance, on page 132, for example, has quite a few preservable plants.

For instance, **geraniums** can be pulled out and some of the soil shaken off the roots. Then the plant can be hung upside down in a basement or cold room to dry. In the spring, the plant can be potted up, trimmed and watered. It's even possible to take cuttings and start new plants from the resuscitated mother plant.

**Creeping Jenny** (lysimachia nummularia) is a perennial, so you can transplant it outside, or take cuttings or both. It's very tough, so expect to see it again in the spring. Mind you, tough as it is, there is not much chance it will survive in its container outside. It has to go into the ground.

The **dracaena** can be kept as a house plant or, again, placed in a basement or cold room, but in a pot, and watered very occasionally, only if you remember. It will revive in the spring. Actually, I've never tried it, but I'll bet that you could conserve **Creeping Jenny** in exactly the same way.

So a lot of Summer Extravagance can be preserved for consumption the next season. Certainly, there aren't many pots in the recipe section that contain so many preservable plants, but keep in mind that any perennial or biannual can be saved. Violas, pansies and dianthus are all biannuals and have a good chance of coming back again the following spring, even before all the snow is gone. If you want to, late in the season transplant the biannuals into the garden, keeping as much soil around the roots as possible. The less you disturb the roots, the better the chance of success. Again, don't think you can get these to survive in the container, outside. In the cold north it's not very likely.

## HOUSE PLANTS:

Wouldn't it be great if you could bring your apple tree into the house and pick apples from it during the long, cold winter? Well, you can't eat ivy but you can enjoy its greenery all year round.

Some plants used in containers are also houseplants so if you buy any for your pots, bring them in during the fall. **English ivy** and **German ivy** are two that come to mind. Now, if these plants have spent the summer in mixed plantings, their roots will be all tied up with other plants' roots. It would be best to transplant them into a home of their own, or to take cuttings. If you decide to transplant them, trim them severely. Be ruthless. I'm talking trimming back the plant at least halfway, to match the trimming you probably gave the roots when you dug the plant out of its original pot.

If you decide to keep the whole plant, there's no need to take cuttings right away. You can wait for late winter or early spring to do that.

To take cuttings, cut a stem section close to a leaf joint. Snip off a few leaves, then stick the stem in a enough damp vermiculite or soil or sand to cover the whole stem right up to the first set of leaves. You can angle it in if you like. I don't recommend just water as there's more chance the cutting will rot in water; also, transplanting a cutting that's been living in clear water into soil can be quite a shock for it. Sand and vermiculite are the best rooting media.

Some plants aren't meant to be houseplants but end up fooling just about everybody! Take good old **impatiens** for example. It does very well in the house. Mind you, if you don't have a sunny window where it can soak up the rays, it will get straggly. Trim it when you bring it in, and pinch off the top growth often. Trim again, and again. Pinch and trim. Keep trimming.

I've tried bringing in **lobelia** and it was fine; and it was in pretty sad shape when I brought it in. Give it lots of light and as above, pinch and trim!

A friend has a very sunny room where she overwinters her **Purple Wave petunia**. It doesn't bloom all winter, but it looks fine – just trim and pinch.

You can bring in a **tomato** plant or two if you've got a good hot spot, a south-facing window helps it thrive. Cherry tomatoes work well but all tomatoes produce if well fed. But, remember, those plants will eventually wear out, so get yourself some new tomatoes in the spring and start all over again!

**Begonias** will survive all winter long in the house. They'll quit blooming after a while and, quite frankly, after November they'll look pretty tired, but they will live. I know, because my daughter, who never thought much of houseplants or any other plant most of her life, discovered their beauty all of a sudden and decided to bring in her patio pot to decorate her room. It had a begonia, an English ivy and an impatiens plant. All those plants are still there, one year later, but the begonia didn't bloom this summer and is actually smaller than it was last year (even with the trimming I insisted on giving it).

If you decide to bring in plants and use them as houseplants, please check for pests. In the house there are no predators to keep populations from exploding, so use a magnifying glass. Treat your plants as though they do have bugs – use the pesticide spray recommended on pages 58 and 59. Another option is to give your plants a good brisk shower with cold water, getting your nozzle under the leaves.

Try yellow sticky tags. These are, just as the name implies, little yellow strips coated with glue and attached to a stick that you poke in the ground. You can make these out of any bright yellow paper; staple onto a popsicle stick and coat with vaseline. They work very well at keeping infestations at a minimum.

Whatever plants you bring in, you'll have to feed them. For any plant to do its very best, it has to be fertilized. Use the same old 20-20-20 that you used outside. Experimenting with overwintering plants is full of surprises. It doesn't always work – but it's always fun.

## INCREDIBLE EDIBLES:

It's possible to conserve many types of fruits and vegetables and, true, there are a few ways to preserve plant material. But is there a way to actually consume the flowers we grow, to prepare them in as colorful and interesting and creative a way as we used them in container gardening? The answer is yes.

Many flowers are edible; of course, others are poisonous, so don't go adding any old thing to your salad unless you know for sure. Some of the following I've never tried and some I have and I'm confident in saying that they can add color and flair to many recipes. **Chrysanthemum**, **dianthus**, **geranium**, and **marigold** petals are edible as are **impatiens**, **snapdragon** and **petunia** flowers. And you can gobble up the flowers and the leaves of **violas** and **pansies**. Yes, the giant petals of **begonias** are as delicious as they look.

What exactly can you do with these lovely edibles? Have a petal salad? Actually, I wouldn't suggest that, but you can add any of the above to any kind of salad. They can be used for garnishing anything from a main dish to a side dish to an appetizer to a glass of wine.

For example, use large **begonia** petals rather than lettuce leaves to line the platter on which you'll be displaying your jellied salad. They will impart a slightly citrus flavor and look luscious. Sprinkle **Signet marigold** petals in your punch to give it spice and color. **Marigold** petals can be used as a substitute for saffron and apparently have some medicinal qualities, though I don't claim to know what these may be.

Make tea out of a cupful of **dianthus** petals – it will have a sweet clove flavor.

I've also used a lot of the various leaves and plants mentioned above to decorate cakes and punches. Of course, I cheat. I sugar them. It works well and looks great – it's really impressive. I've used whole **roses** on a baptismal cake and **dianthus** petals sprinkled on a birthday cake. Little **violas** stay intact and work well, too. Try them in a punch.

To sugar flowers and petals follow the recipe on the next page.

# Sugared Flowers

1 egg white
1-2 teaspoons (5-10 mL) of water
$^1/_4$ cup (60 mL) superfine or berry sugar, or ordinary granulated sugar.
  (On small flowers and petals, the superfine sugar – because the
  granules are fine – looks better, but ordinary sugar will also work.)

Beat the egg white lightly with a fork. Stir in the water. With an artist's paint brush, paint the egg mixture onto the flower. Make sure you cover both sides of the petals. Now dip the flower in the sugar. Sprinkle a bit of sugar on the underside of the petals. Place the sugared flowers on a sheet of waxed paper and let dry. Do the petals more or less the same way, using tweezers to handle them. Once the flowers or the petals are dry, use as you wish, again using tweezers to handle them. They not only look pretty, glistening in the light, but they're highly acceptable as a little treat for any sugar addict.

## DRIED GOODS:

Sundried tomatoes taste great, and many other veggies, such as carrots and onions preserve well when dried. Any herb, like basil or sage or thyme, is delightful to have in the kitchen – they all have wonderful scents. Summer's beauty preserves well too. A good way to do it is by pressing and drying.

Pressing is easy to do. **Pansies** and **violas** press well, as do the little **daisies** and almost every other flower except, possibly, marigolds. It's nice to have two sheets of wood to do the pressing in, but a thick catalogue works too. It's what we used when I was a kid, and I still have some flowers and leaves I pressed way back then.

# Pressing Flowers

**2 small plywood pieces, 12" (30 cm) square (or so)**
**sheets of newspaper**
**sheets of white paper**
**bricks, books, stones or any other weight**
**(or 4 wood clamps if you have them)**
**pretty flowers and leaves**

**Here's how you do it:** Lay out 1 piece of plywood, cover with 2 sheets of newspaper. Place a nice white sheet of paper on top of that. Lay your flower or flowers on top of the paper, making sure that they do not overlap. Now cover carefully with another sheet of white paper; then put 2 more pages of newspaper on top of that. Repeat another two or three times, or until you run out of flowers. Finish off with a layer of newspaper. Top with the second piece of plywood. Place your weight or weights on top of the plywood, or clamp together carefully but tightly at each corner with wood clamps. Weights are actually better than wood clamps because the pressure can be applied to the center of the press, rather than mostly at the corners where there is less likely to be plant material.

Change the paper every day for 6 days. It's the paper that soaks up the moisture as the plants dry out, so you need to replace it. After the 6th day, you can leave the press untouched for a few more days before you put your pressed flowers to use.

You can make an arrangement with the pressed blossoms and frame it under glass, or you can carefully glue the blossoms onto writing paper, or onto a ribbon to make a bookmark. Again, there are all kinds of things you can do – the library craft section is your friend.

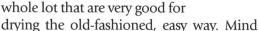

As for dried flowers, that's a whole different story. There's are many ways to do it and a lot of plants to experiment with. Of the plants in this book, there aren't a whole lot that are very good for drying the old-fashioned, easy way. Mind you, any grass dries just fine and so do **helichrysum** (**everlastings**), **dusty miller** and **ivy** – just hang them upside down in an airy place. The new **gypsophila**, **Gypsy** or **Bridal Veil**, don't turn out as well as the old-fashioned white variety, but go ahead and give them a try.

**Dahlias** and **dianthus**, **chrysanthemum** and **matricaria** will dry in drying powder such as silica gel, borax and alum, or sand, which draw out the moisture from the blooms. The type of powder you use depends on how fragile the flower is. **Snowland chrysanthemum** or **violas** and **pansies** and probably **dianthus** will dry well in equal parts of borax and alum. **Dahlias** can be dried in straight sand while **dianthus** and **matricaria Santana** work better in one part sand with two parts borax. Silica gel, the most expensive of the three options, can be used for almost any flower but it should be crushed to form a finer powder for those blossoms that are delicate.

The amount of time the flowers spend in the powder depends a lot on the type of flower, so it's important not to mix heavier flowers with more fragile ones. No matter what the plant, you can expect blooms dried in sand to take the longest to get paper-like, then borax and alum, and the shortest time is in silica gel. **The quicker the flowers dry, the more likely they will keep their original color.**

To use a dessicant, here's what you do:

## Drying Flowers

**an airtight container ( plastic, metal, or even cardboard which
   can be sealed with plastic wrap)
dessicant (enough to cover the bottom to a depth of at least 2" (5cm)
flowers**

**Pour the drying powder into the con-
tainer to a depth of 1" (2. 5cm). Lay
the flowers very gently on the layer
of powder, making sure they do not
touch. Sprinkle more dessicant
over each blossom, coating each
one well. You can use a tooth-
pick or tweezers to separate
petals and get all the nooks
and crannies with the powder. Now pour another inch
(2.5 cm) of dessicant on top
of the flowers. Store in a
warm, dry place until flowers
are thoroughly dried.**

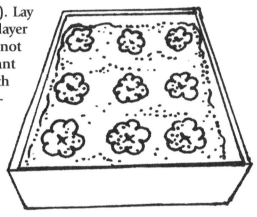

When the flowers are dry you can use them in bouquets or wreaths or crafts.
It's all up to you.

My favorite way of drying is one I use to make potpourri. When I deadhead
my plants, or if I have a bouquet of fresh flowers that's just about done, I just
leave the flower heads in a cardboard box till they dry. Then, I strip off the
petals and add them to a glass vase that sits on the dining room table. Every
once in a while, I add a drop of rose essence to the whole thing and shake it
up. **Geranium** petals, **pansies**, **dianthus** petals, and **roses**, of course, all have
a nice fragrance and work well. When my vase gets full, I use some of my potpourri in small open containers to decorate a bedroom or a bathroom or any
other room in the house. Sometimes, I give some of it away or I sew some up
in pretty little bags to use as sachets in drawers or closets. It's a simple way of
bringing the outdoors in!

## CANNED GOODS

Tomatoes in a jar look sooo edible. They were really fresh when they were canned but, even if they look and taste great, they're quite a bit different than when they were in the garden. The same but different; like a snapshot of the real thing.

Should you be canning dahlias? Dahlias in a jar? I don't think so. Dahlias on a jar? Maybe. Dahlias over a jar? You bet. Especially when it's a framed photograph. Keep that beautiful begonia or petunia or marigold forever, with pictures. That can open up a whole new hobby and a lot of new possibilities. Plant photography can be very specialized, but even an amateur can come up with some very preservable photos. Framed close-ups of gorgeous bouquets can decorate any room in the house, and what a great way to hang on to a favorite floral display.

You can also take your best photos, go to a printer and get a calendar made up for yourself or as gifts for family and friends. Let your pictures tell the story.

You know how, sometimes, when you think of cheesecake, your mouth waters and you can almost taste it? There is no cake there, but in your mind it is very clear – it exists. That's the way it is with flowers, too. The best way to preserve and conserve summer and its floriferous bounty is to engrave the images in your mind. Always with me are grandma's velvety gloxinia, sitting pretty on her kitchen table; I have close-ups of my sister's and my little fingers manipulating the snaps to make them roar; I have visions of pansies dancing all along the front of grandma's house; and, of course, there are vivid memories of stately gladiola, that I helped grandma cut, decorating the nearby little mission church.

I hope I've been able to give you a few ideas on how to enjoy summer all year long. Our spring and summer seasons are short but intense, and full of magic! Seeing those spindly new plants grow into strong, healthy specimens, then bloom in a rainbow of colors, is always a surprise and a miracle. Winter and its storms and cold just don't exist. Doing up containers and otherwise creating and playing with nature is truly a gift. Feast and partake!

# EVERYDAY FAVORITES –

## 101 recipes for outrageously beautiful pots and planters

# Sunny Morsels

The lobelia peeks through the petunias and fills in the empty spaces as well as trailing over the edge. This works well as it keeps the roots of the lobelia cool, so that it thrives under warmer conditions than it otherwise would.

*Suggested serving:* 10-12" (25-30 cm) hanging or patio pot

*Temperature:* shade, part sun; low to moderate heat

| *Ingredients:* | | *10-12" (25-30 cm)* |
|---|---|---|
| ✤ lobelia, trailing, sapphire | 1 | |
| ✵ petunias, single, pink, salmon, rose or red | 3 | |

*At serving time:* Cut back lobelia if it gets scraggly, see the TIP on page 71. Deadhead the petunias as desired.

**TIP . . .**
**Lobelia** is transplanted in bunches of 3 to 6 plants depending on the transplanting method. If you want just a touch of lobelia, choose a smaller bunch. You can also divide a bunch into two. Or if you like, choose a big bunch – which is what you would want in this recipe.

*Pictured on page 34.*

# Dainty Bites

This superb pot dishes out color with the impatiens; the lobelia adds flair. The overall effect is one of elegance and good taste.

*Suggested serving:* 10-12" (25-30 cm) hanging or patio pot

*Temperature:* shade, part shade; low to moderate heat

| *Ingredients:* | | *10-12" (25-30 cm)* |
|---|---|---|
| ✤ impatiens, double | 1 | |
| ✵ impatiens, mix, 6" (15 cm) | 3 | |
| ★ lobelia, trailing or upright (optional in 10" [25 cm] pot), sapphire or rose | 3 | |

*At serving time:* Deadhead as desired. Trim the lobelia when it starts to look tired. See the TIP in the following recipe.

### TIP . . .

It's next to impossible to deadhead **impatiens**, so what I suggest is to just brush off the dead petals with your hand.

*Pictured on page 86.*


# Élégance

The masses of tiny blossoms of the lobelia are a strong match for the large begonia blossoms in this class act. Try doing up a pot in all white for a lacy bridal look, or use a mixture of colors to make up a spicy pot.

*Suggested serving:* 10-12" (25-30 cm) hanging pot or
        10-14" (25-35 cm) patio pot

*Temperature:* shade, part sun, sun; low to moderate heat

| *Ingredients:* | *10-12"* *(25-30 cm)* | *12-14"* *(30-35 cm)* |
|---|---|---|
| ✤ begonias, non-stop, one color or a mix | 2 | 3 |
| ☆ lobelia, trailing, one color | 2 | 3 |

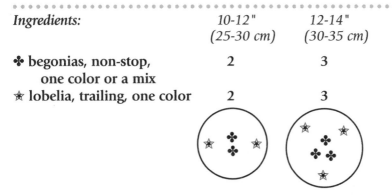

*At serving time:* Deadhead as desired.  For begonia TIPS, see pages 82, 89 and 97.

### TIP . . .

With **lobelia**, you can't very well deadhead each flower, so you simply give it a good haircut. Trimming off about a third of the plant in early August will ensure it blooms till frost. This is especially important if the pot is in full sun; in shade the trimming should not be necessary.

*Pictured on page 33.*

# Caribbean Lace

The rosy-peach diascia defines daintiness and contrasts well with the bold lines of the dark burgundy petunia. The two ingredients combine to look soft and lacy, with just a hint of tropic spice.

*Suggested serving:* 10-12" (25-30 cm) hanging pot or
10-14" (25-35 cm) patio pot

*Temperature:* shade, part sun, sun; low to high heat

| Ingredients: | 10" (25 cm) | 12" (30 cm) | 14" (35 cm) |
|---|---|---|---|
| ♣ petunias, single, burgundy | 1 | 2 | 3 |
| ✴ diascia | 3 | 4 | 4 |

*At serving time:* Deadhead as needed. Do not put the diascia too close to the edges – it really spreads.

*Pictured on page 51.*


# Pretty in Pink

Both the miniature pastel-pink petunia and the white alyssum are so delicate that this arrangement has a light and airy allure.

*Suggested serving:* 10-12" (25-30 cm) hanging pot or
10-14" (25-35 cm) patio pot

*Temperature:* part sun, sun; low to moderate heat

| Ingredients: | 10-14" (25-35 cm) |
|---|---|
| ♣ petunias, Fantasy Pink Morn | 3 |
| ✴ alyssum, white | 3 |

# Pretty in Pink continued

*At serving time:* Deadhead as desired; trim alyssum as needed. See TIP below.

**TIP ...**

You can no more deadhead **alyssum** than you can lobelia – the florets are miniature. Actually, it does very well unless there's a heat wave, when it may decide to go to seed; in that case, trim off about a third of the plant. That's right, just shave it off. It will reward you by growing with renewed vigor and will be smothered by little white florets once again. If you have a special event in the latter part of August, trim the alyssum in very late July and your pot will be exquisite when you need it.

*Pictured on pages 33 and 34.*


# Salmon Simplicity

With salmon petunias and blue lobelia there is no exotic splash of color here; it's the simplicity that makes this pot more than palatable.

*Suggested serving:* 10-12" (25-30 cm) hanging pot or
10-14" (25-35 cm) patio pot

*Temperature:* shade, part sun; moderate to low heat

| Ingredients: | 10"<br>*(25 cm)* | 12-14"<br>*(30-35 cm)* |
|---|---|---|
| ✤ petunias, single, salmon | 2 | 3 |
| ✦ lobelia, trailing, sapphire | 2 | 2 |
| ★ lobelia, upright, sapphire<br>    or white | 2 | 2 |

*At serving time:* Deadhead as desired; trim lobelia if it gets scraggly, see the TIP on page 71.

**Variations:** Use all **trailing** or all **upright lobelia** if you prefer.

*Pictured on page 51.*

# Grape Delight

The petunias and the lobelia, both lilac, contrast with each other by size and texture, giving zest to the deep purple petunias.

*Suggested serving:* 10-12" (25-30 cm) hanging pot or
10-14" (25-35 cm) patio pot

*Temperature:* shade, part sun; low to moderate heat

| Ingredients: | | *10-14" (25-35 cm)* |
|---|---|---|
| ❖ petunias, single, purple | 2 | |
| ✷ petunias, single, lilac | 2 | |
| ★ lobelia, trailing, lilac | 3 | |

*At serving time:* Trim lobelia if it starts to look weary, see the TIP on page 71. This pot will take sun but remember, lobelia doesn't like it hot!

*Pictured on page 34.*

# Easter Egg Special

The burgundy in this new double petunia is rich and velvety and blooms quite profusely. Try this combination for a different and pretty look.

*Suggested serving:* 10-12" (25-30 cm) hanging pot or
10-14" (25-35 cm) patio pot

*Temperature:* shade, part sun, sun; low to moderate heat

| Ingredients: | *10"* *(24 cm)* | *12"* *(30 cm)* | *14"* *(35 cm)* |
|---|---|---|---|
| ❖ petunia, double cascade, burgundy | 1 | 2 | 3 |
| ✷ alyssum, mixed | 4 | 6 | 6 |

# Easter Egg Special continued

*At serving time:* Deadhead the petunias; trim if necessary, as doubles may tend to stretch. Trim the alyssum as per TIP, page 73.

*Pictured on page 52 and 120.*

# Dainty Treat

This simple but effective combination has the soft pastel-pink of the geranium and petunias off-set by the lively purple pansy.

*Suggested serving:* 10-12" (25-30 cm) hanging pot or
10-14" (25-35 cm) patio pot

*Temperature:* shade, part sun, sun; low to moderate heat

| *Ingredients:* | *10"* *(25 cm)* | *12-14"* *(30-35 cm)* |
|---|---|---|
| ❖ geranium, zonal, light pink | 1 | 1 |
| ✵ petunias, Fantasy Pink Morn | 2 | 3 |
| ★ pansy, Purple Rain | 2 | 3 |

*At serving time:* Deadhead as desired.

## TIP ...

**Pansies** and **violas** won't bloom if you put them in too deep, so when you're transplanting make sure you don't cover the crown. (By the way, the crown is where the stem and the leaves meet the root.)

*Pictured on page 51.*

# Dew Drops

This versatile arrangement looks great in any corner! The verbena peeks through the maze of color while the dianthus gives an air of distinction.

*Suggested serving:* 10-12" (25-30 cm) hanging pot or
10-14" (25-35 cm) patio pot

*Temperature:* shade, part sun, sun; low to moderate heat

*Ingredients:*                       *10-14" (25-35 cm)*

❖ verbena, Imagination         2
✴ dianthus, any color           2
★ pansies, Purple Rain          2

*At serving time:* Deadhead as desired. See the TIP on page 75.

## TIP ...
When deadheading **dianthus**, you can trim off the individual flower, or wait until most of the florets have wilted, then cut off the whole branch.

*Pictured on page 52.*

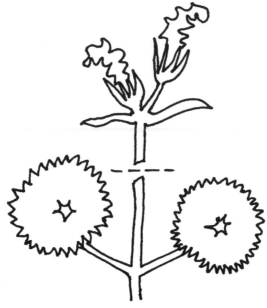

# Plum Pudding

What a variety in one pot! There is lots of color here; the plum and purple petunias provide harmony; the yellow pansies give contrast; the alyssum adds texture.

*Suggested serving:* 10-12" (25-30 cm) hanging pot or
10-16" (25-40 cm) patio pot

*Temperature:* shade, part sun, sun; low to moderate heat

| Ingredients: | 10" (25 cm) | 12" (30 cm) | 14-16" (35-40 cm) |
|---|---|---|---|
| ✤ petunias, Madness Plum Crazy | 1 | 1 | 3 |
| ☆ petunias, Fantasy Midnight | 2 | 3 | 3 |
| ★ pansies, clear yellow | 2 | 3 | 4 |
| ✳ alyssum, purple | 2 | 3 | 4 |

*At serving time:* Deadhead as desired. See the TIP on page 73 about alyssum and the TIP on page 75 for information on pansies.

*Pictured on page 33.*

# Apricot and Peach Salad

The peaches and cream of the geranium and the verbena are marbled with the purple petunia, making for an interesting and chic look.

*Suggested serving:* 10-12" (25-30 cm) hanging pot or
14-16" (35-40 cm) patio pot

*Temperature:* shade, part sun, sun: low to high heat

| *Ingredients:* | 10-12"<br>(25-30 cm) | 14-16"<br>(35-40 cm) |
|---|---|---|
| ✤ geranium, zonal,<br>    peachy pink, old rose,<br>    or salmon colored | 1 | 2 |
| ☆ petunia, Fantasy Midnight | 2 | 3 |
| ★ verbena, apricot | 2 | 3 |

*At serving time:* Deadhead as needed.

**Variations:** Use **Fantasy Crystal Red petunias** rather than **Fantasy Midnight**, for a softer look.

*Pictured on page 51.*


# Dream Puff

This arrangement is like a puffy cloud with a bit of sunshine coming through, with its deep purple and soft lilac petunias and its sunny daisies.

*Suggested serving:* 10-12" (25-30 cm) hanging pot or
10-16" (25-40 cm) patio pot

*Temperature:* part shade, sun; moderate to high heat

# Dream Puff   continued

| Ingredients: | 10-14"<br>(25-35 cm) | 16"<br>(40 cm) |
|---|---|---|
| ✤ petunia, single, lilac | 1 | 3 |
| ✹ petunia, Fantasy Midnight | 3 | 3 |
| ★ Dahlberg daisies, Golden Fleece | 3 | 3 |

*At serving time:* Deadhead as desired.


# Peach Punch

Peaches with cream has long been one of my favorites, and this pot is a prime example of great taste! The peach of the geranium and the verbena is mild and the texture provided by the zinnia adds a bit of zing.

*Suggested serving:* 10-12" (25-30 cm) hanging pot
10-16" (25-40 cm) patio pot

*Temperature:* part sun, sun; moderate to high heat

| Ingredients: | 10-12"<br>(25-30 cm) | 14-16"<br>(35-40 cm) |
|---|---|---|
| ✤ geranium, zonal, peachy pink,<br>old rose, or salmon colored | 1 | 2 |
| ✹ verbena, apricot | 2 | 3 |
| ★ zinnia, Crystal White | 2 | 3 |

*At serving time:* Deadhead as desired. Do not overwater!

*Pictured on page 51 and 86.*

79

# Partly Pink

The dianthus, with its various shades of pink, create a lacy effect while the violas spice up the whole affair.

*Suggested serving:* 10-12" (25-30 cm) hanging pot or
10-18" (25-45 cm) patio pot

*Temperature:* shade, part sun, sun; low to moderate heat

| *Ingredients:* | *10-14"* *(25-35 cm)* | *16-18"* *(40-45 cm)* |
|---|---|---|
| ♣ petunia, single, pink | 1 | 3 |
| ★ dianthus, Diamond Blush Pink | 3 | 3 |
| ✰ violas, mixed | 3 | 3 |

*At serving time:* Deadhead as desired. See violas TIP on page 75 and the TIP on page 76 for trimming dianthus.

*Pictured on page 33.*


# Peach Custard

The dainty diascia has such a light texture that it seems to float around the geraniums and the petunias. The fluffy white alyssum gives a contrast in texture, as well as color.

*Suggested serving:* 10-12" (25-30 cm) hanging pot or
10-18" (25-45) patio pot

*Temperature:* shade, part sun, sun; moderate heat

# Peach Custard    continued

| Ingredients: | 10"<br>(25 cm) | 12-14"<br>(30-35 cm) | 16-18"<br>(40-45 cm) |
|---|---|---|---|
| ✤ geranium, zonal, salmon | 1 | 1 | 3 |
| ✳ diascia | 1 | 1 | 2 |
| ★ petunia, Fantasy Crystal Red | 2 | 3 | 3 |
| ✱ alyssum, white | 2 | 3 | 3 |

*At serving time:* Deadhead as desired. To trim alyssum, see TIP page 73.

### TIP ...

Put the **diascia** as close to the geraniums as you can. It has a wide spread and, when put in this way, it seems to float up from nowhere.

*Pictured on page 33.*

# Spritzy Morsel

The white alyssum sets off the contrasting pink and the velvety purple, making this pot simple yet colorful.

*Suggested serving:* 10-14" (25-35 cm) upright or hanging pot

*Temperature:* part sun; sun

| Ingredients: | 10-12"<br>(25-30 cm) | 14-16"<br>(35-40 cm) |
|---|---|---|
| ✤ petunia, single, pink or salmon | 1 | 3 |
| ✳ petunia, Fantasy Midnight or purple | 3 | 3 |
| ★ alyssum, white | 3 | 3 |

*At serving time:* Deadhead as desired. To trim alyssum, see TIP on page 73.

*Pictured on pages 34 and 85.*

# Taste of Paradise

Nothing can surpass the delectable Giant begonia in beauty or in size! The huge flowing flowers add exquisite beauty and color wherever they are.

*Suggested serving:* 10-14" (25-35 cm) hanging pot
10-16" (25-40 cm) patio pot

*Temperature:* shade, part sun; low to moderate heat

| *Ingredients:* | 10"<br>*(25 cm)* | 12"<br>*(30 cm)* | 14-16"<br>*(35-40 cm)* |
|---|---|---|---|
| ✤ begonias, American Giant,<br>  pendulous or upright,<br>  one color, or a mix | 1 | 2 | 3 |

*At serving time:* Deadhead occasionally; see TIPS on pages 89 and 97.

**TIP ...**
**Begonias** tend to show off their blooms in the direction that the leaves point. If you want show all around, plant the begonias in opposite directions, with the leaves pointing outward, over the edge of the pot.

*Pictured on page 120.*

# Dream Drop

The long, flowing silver lotus vine seems to drip all around the colorful geraniums. Though it's simple to whip up, it remains a visual delicacy.

*Suggested serving:* 12" (30 cm) hanging pot

*Temperature:* part sun, sun; moderate to high heat

# Dream Drop    continued

- - - - - - - - - - - - - - - - - - - - - - - - - - - - - - - - - - - - - - -

*Ingredients:*                    *12" (30 cm)*

✤ lotus vine                    1
✶ ivy geraniums, one color      3
    or a mixture

*At serving time:* Water every day, occasionally watering right through, but usually just enough to keep the soil evenly moist.

### TIP ...

Both the **geraniums** and **lotus vine** like even moisture. If the tips of the vine start to turn yellow, it's telling you to check your watering habits. The best way to do that is to poke your finger 1-2" (2.5-5 cm) into the soil. If it feels muddy, let it dry out. If the surface is damp but it's fairly dry underneath, add water accordingly, then it will return to it's old silvery self.

*Pictured on page 119.*


# Ring of Fire

Hot and spicy, with bold deep red petunias and fiery yellow daisies.

*Suggested serving:* 12" (30 cm) hanging pot or
                     12-14" (30-35 cm) patio pot

*Temperature:* part sun, sun; low to high heat

- - - - - - - - - - - - - - - - - - - - - - - - - - - - - - - - - - - - - - -

*Ingredients:*                    *12-14" (30-35 cm)*

✤ petunias, single, red          3
✶ Dahlberg daisies,              3
    Golden Fleece

*At serving time:* Deadhead petunias as desired, the daisies as needed.

**Variation:** If it's an upright pot you're making (not a hanging version), put a small **dracaena spike** in the center.

*Pictured on page 33.*

# Burgundy Drama

The creamy yellow lights up the rich burgundy, making this pot as dramatic as Betty Davis' eyes!

*Suggested serving:* 12" (30 cm) hanging pot or
12-14" (30-35 cm) patio pot

*Temperature:* part sun, sun; low to moderate heat

* * * * * * * * * * * * * * * * * * * * * * * * * * * * * * * * * * * * * * * * * * * * * * * * * * * * * * * * * * * *

| *Ingredients:* | *12-14" (30-35 cm)* |
|---|---|
| ✤ petunia, single, yellow | 1 |
| ✳ petunia, single, burgundy | 3 |
| ★ alyssum, apricot | 4 |

*At serving time:* Trim the alyssum when it starts going to seed. See the TIP on page 73. Deadhead as desired. Trim petunias if they get out of hand.

**Variation:** Add a **dracaena spike** to the middle of the pot, if if isn't the hanging version.

*Pictured on page 33.*

| 1 | *Spritzy Morsel, 10" (25 cm), page 81* |
|---|---|
| 2 | *Summer Basket, page 92* |
| 3 | *Fire-Glow, page 140* |
| 4 | *Shy Show, page 125* |
| 5 | *Fricassée, page 132* |
| 6 | *Royal Icing, page 99* |
| 7 & 8 | *Simplicity, 12" (30 cm) and 16" (41 cm), page 88* |

# Salmon Mousse

The purple flowers and fine leaves of the verbena peek through, weaving around the petunias, adding contrast in color and texture.

*Suggested serving:* 12" (30 cm) hanging pot or
12-14" (30-35 cm) patio pot

*Temperature:* shade, part shade, sun; moderate to high heat

*Ingredients:*            *12-14" (30-35 cm)*

| | |
|---|---|
| ❖ verbena, Imagination | 1 |
| ✶ petunias, single, salmon or pink | 4 |

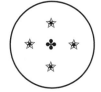

*At serving time:* Deadhead as needed.

*Pictured on page 120.*

1  *Peach Punch, page 79*
2  *Dainty Bites, page 70*
3  *Tutti Frutti, page 131*
4  *Party Punch, page 129*
5  *Confetti Concoction, page 104*
6  *Pot of Gold, page 118*

# Simplicity

It doesn't take all that much to dress up a petunia – they're all quite capable of putting on a show on their own. In this pot, the miniature petunias match the regular-sized perfectly and the alyssum, as a side dish, is a nice treat.

*Suggested serving:* 12" ( 30 cm ) hanging pot or
12-16" ( 30-40 cm) patio pot

*Temperature:* shade, part sun, sun; moderate to high heat

| Ingredients | 12" (30 cm) | 14-16" (35-40 cm) |
|---|---|---|
| ♣ petunias, single, veined salmon | 1 | 3 |
| ✴ petunias, Fantasy Crystal Red | 3 | 3 |
| ★ alyssum, white, apricot or purple (optional) | 3 | 3 |

*At serving time:* Deadhead as desired. Trim the alyssum if needed, see the TIP on page 73.

*Pictured on page 85.*

# Strawberry Sunday

The pink begonia is all dressed up in it's Sunday best, swirling in impatiens and dripping with lobelia. The ivy gives the finishing touch.

*Suggested serving:* 12" (30 cm) hanging pot or
14-16" (35-40 cm) patio pot

*Temperature:* shade, part sun; low to moderate heat

| Ingredients: | 12-14"<br>(30-35 cm) | 16"<br>(40 cm) |
|---|---|---|
| ♣ begonias, Non-Stop, pink or rose | 1 | 3 |
| ✶ impatiens, Pink Swirl | 3 | 3 |
| ★ lobelia, trailing, sapphire | 2 | 2 |
| ✳ ivy, English | 1 | 1 |

*At serving time:* Deadhead as needed. See the TIPS on pages 82 and 97. See the TIP on page 95 about ivy and the illustration on page 144 about trimming.

*Variation:* Use an **American Giant** rather than a **Non-Stop begonia** in an upright pot. You can also skip the **ivy** and just put in an extra **lobelia** plant.

## TIP . . .
Trim off the single **begonia** blossoms to get larger double flowers.

*Pictured on page 51.*

# Hoopla

This red, white and blue pot is vibrant in color and ready for a parade! The brachycome (Swan River Daisy) adds a festive air to an already hot pot!

*Suggested serving:* 12" ( 30 cm) hanging pot or
12-18 (30-45 cm) patio pot

*Temperature:* part sun, sun; low to moderate heat

| Ingredients: | 12-14"<br>(30-35 cm) | 16-18"<br>(40-45 cm) |
|---|---|---|
| ✤ petunias, single, purple | 1 | 3 |
| ✮ petunias, Fantasy Red | 3 | 3 |
| ★ alyssum, white | 3 | 3 |
| ✳ brachycome, purple | 3 | 3 |

*At serving time:* Deadhead the petunias and the brachycome as needed. Trim the alyssum if it goes to seed, see the TIP on page 73.

# Fancy Pansy

A roly-poly ball of blue and pink with the fresh-faced pansies spicing up the perky impatiens.

*Suggested serving:* 10" (25 cm) wire basket

*Temperature:* shade, part sun, low to moderate heat

| Ingredients: | 10" (25 cm) |
|---|---|
| ✣ pansies, clear blue | 12 |
| ✳ impatiens, mixed | 12 |

*At serving time:* See the planting TIP on page 75. Deadhead as desired.

## TIP ...

My sketch is a bit like a world map that stretches out a round planet on a flat paper; its a bit deceiving. The centre is the top portion of the pot. The next circle represents the top row of plants along the outside of the pot and about a quarter of the way down. Just imagine that the center line runs around the middle of the pot.

The third row, which stretches the plants far apart in the diagram, is actually the smallest part of the basket and about three quarters of the way down. In reality, when you put in this row, the plants are closer together than those above them. Do not plant too close to the bottom and don't worry, the plants will fill in.

To complicate matters, you'll be planting the outside row, (the bottom row of plants) first; then the centre row and last, you'll do up the top – or middle of the map.

It really is less complicated than it sounds believe me. The first pot will be the most difficult.

*Pictured on page 119.*

# Summer Basket

This color-ball will liven up any corner; of course petunias do well in almost every situation, so you are assured of great performance by this live-wire!

*Suggested serving:* 10" (25 cm) wire basket

*Temperature:* shade, part sun, sun; moderate to high heat

| Ingredients: | 10" (25 cm) |
|---|---|
| ✤ petunia, single, any color | 1 |
| ✶ petunias, Fantasy Mix | 12 |

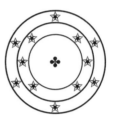

*At serving time:* See the planting TIP on page 91 before you begin. Deadhead as needed.

*Pictured on page 85.*

# Melba Sauce

This mystical mixture looks like a nest for the fairies. It's a jumble of purple and peachy pink with a an interesting texture!

*Suggested serving:* 12" (30 cm) wire basket

*Temperature:* shade, part sun, sun; low to moderate heat

| Ingredients: | 12" (30 cm) |
|---|---|
| ✤ verbena Imagination | 7 |
| ✶ diascia | 10 |

*At serving time:* See the planting TIP on page 91. Deadhead as desired.

# Zabaglione

Truly beautiful! The puffs of white alyssum are surrounded by various shades of fibrous begonias and topped with a lovely Non-Stop begonia.

*Suggested Serving:* 12"(30 cm) wire basket

*Temperature:* shade, part sun; low to moderate heat

*Ingredients:*                    *12" (30 cm)*

❖ begonia, Non-Stop, pink,        1
   peach, yellow, rose or white
★ begonias, fibrous, mixed        12
   colors
✶ alyssum, white                  3

*At serving time:* See the planting TIP on page 91 before you begin. Then check out TIPS on pages 82, 89, 97 about begonias and the TIP on page 73 about alyssum.

*Pictured on page 34.*

# Mumbo Jumbo Jambalaya

The extra effort is worthwhile to achieve this dramatic display. You couldn't vary the ingredients much more than this, nor could you get more of a mix in texture and color.

*Suggested serving:* 16" (40 cm) wire basket

*Temperature:* part sun, sun; moderate heat

| *Ingredients:* | *16" (40 cm)* |
|---|---|
| ❖ ivy geranium, red | 1 |
| ✴ thunbergia, mixed | 3 |
| ★ zinnias, Crystal White | 3 |
| ✳ petunias, Fantasy Red | 6 |
| ✻ marigolds, signet, Gem golden, yellow, orange or tangerine | 6 |
| ✦ ageratum, 6-8" (15-20 cm) | 6 |

*At serving time:* See the planting tip on page 91 before you begin. Deadhead as desired; keep evenly moist. If you want the thunbergia to climb as well as trail, wind a vine around the wires of the hanger.

# Fresh Mélange

The Imagination verbena competes well with the vigorous Wave petunia and breaks up its color with a squirt of purple.

*Suggested serving:* 16-20" (40-50 cm) wire basket

*Temperature:* shade, part sun, sun; moderate to high heat

*Ingredients:*          *16-20" (40-50 cm)*

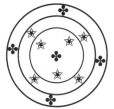

❖ petunias, Wave,            6
    Rose, pink, Misty Lilac
    or coral
✫ verbena, Imagination       7

*At serving time:* See the planting TIP on page 91 before your begin. Deadhead as needed.

*Pictured on page 52.*

# Layer Cake

The petunias are transplanted in layers, the whole depth of the pot. The end result is a magnificent color-ball that looks great anywhere!

*Suggested serving:* 18-22" (45-55 cm) wire basket

*Temperature:* shade, part sun, sun; moderate to high heat

*Ingredients:*          *18-22" (45-55 cm)*

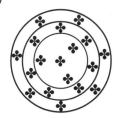

❖ petunias, single, one color     18
    or a mix of colors

*At serving time:* See the planting tip on page 91 before you begin. Deadhead as desired.

*Pictured on the front cover.*

# Fruit Roll

Fresh and friendly, this basket is the belle of the ball! Both the coleus and the dusty miller have a velvety texture to their broad leaves that contrast well with the fine foliage and flowers of the marigolds and the tiny lobelia. The Purple Rain pansy pours over the edge, with its yellow eye picking up the burnt yellow of the begonia.

*Suggested serving:* 18-20" (45-50 cm) wire basket

*Temperature:* shade, part shade; low to moderate heat

| Ingredients: | 18-20" (45-50 cm) |
|---|---|
| ❖ begonia, American Giant, Sunburst | 1 |
| ✴ pansies, Purple Rain | 2 |
| ★ ivies, English | 2 |
| ✳ nemesia, white or mix | 2 |
| ◆ dusty miller, Cirrus | 3 |
| ✳ coleus | 3 |
| ☆ lobelia, trailing, sapphire | 5 |
| ✳ marigold, signet | 5 |

*At serving time:* See the planting tip on pages 91 and 75 before you begin. Deadhead as desired, see the TIP on page 71. Trim off some of the Purple Rain if it gets overgrown.

## TIP . . .

When choosing an **ivy**, check out how many plants in the pot. Take the one with the most plants, or with the most branches.

# Pinch of Spice

This verbena does love the shade. Its fine flowers and leaves add spice to the begonia. Still, it stands back and lets the floriferous American Giant lead the show.

*Suggested serving:* 14-16" (35-40 cm) by 8" (20 cm) wide by approximately 10" (25 cm) deep wall-mount basket.

*Temperature:* shade, part sun; low to moderate heat

*Ingredients:*                     *14-16" (35-40 cm)*

♣ verbena, Imagination          1
✯ begonia, American Giant,       1
    pendulous, any color

*At serving time:* Deadhead as desired; read up on begonias in TIP pages 82 and 89.

### TIP . . .

Some plants, such as **begonias**, do not like wet feet. What that means is that you should definitely let the top of the soil dry out between waterings; when you do water, water well. Following these simple instructions will help avoid soil borne and/or fungal diseases.

# Smart Tart

The ivy geranium looks smart and is easy to grow. Like its upright relative, it blasts with color. Garnish with alyssum to complete the ensemble.

*Suggested serving:* 14-16" (35-40 cm) by 8" (20 cm) across and approximately 10" (25 cm) deep wall-mount container.

*Temperature:* shade, part sun, sun; moderate heat

| *Ingredients:* | *14-16" (35-40 cm)* |
| --- | --- |
| ✤ ivy geranium, any color | 1 |
| ✦ alyssum, white | 2 |

*At serving time:* Deadhead as needed. Trim alyssum if it starts going to seed, see the TIP on page 53.

**Variation:** If you have a really hot spot, or if you happen to like the splash of **portulaca**, use 2 portulaca plants rather than the alyssum.


# Trailing Joy

The flowing lobelia spreads, filling in all the empty spaces, and it is a great backdrop to the impatiens' blooms.

*Suggested serving:* 8-10" (20-25 cm) by 6" (15 cm) wide by approximately 6" (15 cm) deep wall-mount container or 12-16" (30-40 cm) by 8" (20 cm) wide and approximately 10" (25 cm) deep wall-mount container

*Temperature:* shade, part sun; moderate heat

| *Ingredients:* | *8-10"* *(20-25 cm)* | *12-16"* *(30-40 cm)* |
| --- | --- | --- |
| ✤ lobelia, trailing, any color | 1 | 1 |
| ✦ impatiens, any color, any height | 1 | 3 |

*At serving time:* Deadhead as desired. See the TIP on page 71.

# Royal Icing

This little pot, with the dahlia standing royally in the center, keeps its quiet charm even with all its bright marigolds and alyssum.

*Suggested serving:* 12-14" (30-35 cm) color bowl or patio pot

*Temperature:* part sun sun, moderate to high heat

| *Ingredients:* | *12-14" (30-35 cm)* |
|---|---|
| ❖ dahlia, 12-16" (30-40 cm) | 1 |
| ✳ ageratum, purple | 3 |
| ★ marigolds, 8-12" (20-30 cm) | 3 |

*At serving time:* Deadhead whenever a dahlia blossom starts to shed its petals. Trim alyssum as in the TIP on page 73.

## TIP ...

When you're picking out a **dahlia** for this pot, you might notice that some of the plants, though they look healthy, have lighter leaves than others. No, they're not under-nourished; it's just that in some plant varieties, plants that will bloom in light colors have matching leaves. Those that have darker leaves or dark veins in the leaves will likely bloom purple, red or some other dark color. When I tested this pot, I purposely picked out a plant with light leaves and, sure enough, it turned out to be a beautiful pale yellow. **Snapdragons** have that same trait.

*Pictured on page 85.*

# Midnight Stars

This arrangement was inspired by the color of the container – peach. Not many colors suited the pot but the purple hues and the splash of daisies certainly did the trick, and would in any other pot, too. The plum and purple complement each other, and the shades of violet daisies have a soft texture that contrast well with the solid leaves of the petunias.

*Suggested serving:* 12-14" (30-35 cm) color bowl, patio pot or hanging pot.

*Temperature:* shade, part sun, sun; moderate to high heat

| *Ingredients:* | *12-14" (30-35 cm)* |
|---|---|
| ✤ petunia, single orchid or plum | 1 |
| ✭ petunias, single purple | 3 |
| ★ brachycome, mixed | 3 |

*At serving time:* Deadhead as desired. Trim petunias if they begin to stretch (get leggy).

*Pictured on the front cover.*

# Berry and Cherry Dreams

Liven up a shady spot with this main attraction. Hummingbirds and butterflies will visit with glee – that's the effect nicotiana has on nature, with it's sweet scent and star shape.

*Suggested servings:* 12-16" (30-40 cm) color bowl or patio pot.

*Temperature:* shade, part sun; low to moderate heat.

| *Ingredients:* | *12-14"* *(30-35 cm)* | *16"* *(40 cm)* |
|---|---|---|
| ✤ nicotiana, any color, 14-20" (35-50 cm) | 1 | 3 |
| ✭ impatiens, mixed, 6-10" (15-25 cm) | 4 | 6 |

# Berry and Cherry Dreams continued

*At serving time:* Deadhead as desired.  See the TIP on page 71.

**TIP . . .**

Seed companies have come up with **matching mixes** for many different types of flowers, from dianthus to portulaca to petunias and pansies and impatiens – just to name those that come to mind. One has burgundies, pinks and roses with a bit of white while the other is made up of corals, peaches and oranges; another is a mixture of blues and purples. This will simplify life as far as getting the right colors when making up pots. For this particular arrangement, I suggest the Merlot Mix impatiens; this will almost guarantee a good match with the pink, rose, lime or even red of the nicotiana.

Pictured on the back cover.

# Ambrosia

The "poor man's orchid" schizanthus, is in the spotlight applauded by the cheeky pansies and shimmery lobelia. This concoction is especially delicious in the night light.

*Suggested serving:* 12-16" (30-40 cm) color bowl or patio pot

*Temperature:* shade, part sun, sun; moderate heat

*Ingredients:*          *12-16" (30-40 cm)*

❖ schizanthus, any color,     1
    12" (30 cm)
✴ pansies, mixed          3
★ lobelia, upright Crystal Palace   3

*At serving time:* Before you start, see about violas and pansies, TIP page 75, and about lobelia, TIP page 71.

**TIP . . .**

Shaving off a bit of the **schizanthus** will bring on a second coming; simply trim off a few florets all around the plant, keeping its natural rounded shape.

*Pictured on page 119.*

# Spice of Life

This pot includes my all-favorite herb plant, Siam Queen Basil. Not only does it look majestic, it smells terrific. The soft pink of its blossoms doesn't hinder the taste of the herb and contrasts well with its burgundy-green leaves. Of course, don't underestimate the wave of color the petunias and the portulaca give to the whole ensemble.

*Suggested serving:* 12-18" (30-45 cm) color bowl or patio pot

*Temperature:* part sun, sun; moderate to high heat

| *Ingredients:* | 12-14"<br>(30-35 cm) | 16-18"<br>(40-45 cm) |
| --- | --- | --- |
| ✤ basil, Siam Queen | 1 | 1 |
| ✴ portulaca, mixed | 4 | 6 |
| ★ petunia, Fantasy Pink Morn | 2 | 3 |

*At serving time:* Deadhead as needed. Trim basil and use in cooking, if desired.


# Butter Tart

The delectable apricot alyssum takes on the yellow hue of the petunia; the lilac alyssum repeats the lilac of the petunias. The whole is a rich bowlful of pastels.

*Suggested serving:* 12-18" (30-45 cm) color bowl or patio pot

*Temperature:* shade, part sun, sun; moderate heat

# Butter Tart    continued

. . . . . . . . . . . . . . . . . . . . . . . . . . . . . . . . . . . . . . . . . . . . . . . . . . .

| Ingredients: | 12-14"<br>(30-35 cm) | 16-18"<br>(40-45 cm) |
|---|---|---|
| ✤ petunia, single, yellow | 1 | 2 |
| ✧ petunias, single, lilac | 2 | 2 |
| ★ alyssum, lilac | 3 | 4 |
| ✳ alyssum, apricot | 3 | 4 |

*At serving time:* Deadhead as desired. See the TIP on page 71 for alyssum.

*Pictured on page 52.*

# Scrambled Eggs

The variations in texture and color are what make this pot. The white mass of lobelia surrounds the yolk-yellow pansies.

*Suggested serving:* 12-18" (25-45 cm) color bowl or patio pot

*Temperature:* shade, part sun, sun; low to moderate heat

. . . . . . . . . . . . . . . . . . . . . . . . . . . . . . . . . . . . . . . . . . . . . . . . . . .

| Ingredients: | 12-14"<br>(30-35 cm) | 16-18"<br>(40-45 cm) |
|---|---|---|
| ✤ pansies, yellow | 3 | 5 |
| ✧ lobelia, trailing or upright,<br>    white | 4 | 6 |

*At serving time:* Deadhead as needed. See the TIP on page 75 about pansies. Trim the lobelia if it gets scraggly, see the TIP on page 71.

**Variation:** For alternate ingredients, try 8-12" (20- 30 cm) yellow **snapdragons** rather than the **pansies**.

# Confetti Concoction

The baby's breath is like a cloud of confetti bursting over the sides of the pot, accentuating the quiet blue pansies. The bridal dahlia shows up front and center with its large blossoms.

*Suggested serving:* 12-20" (30-50 cm) color bowl or patio pot

*Temperature:* part sun, sun; moderate heat

| Ingredients: | 12-16"<br>(30-40 cm) | 18-20"<br>(45-50 cm) |
| --- | --- | --- |
| ❖ dahlia, 12-16" (30-40 cm) | 1 | 3 |
| ✴ gypsophila, (baby's breath)<br>   Bridal Veil or Gypsy | 2 | 3 |
| ★ pansies, clear blue | 2 | 3 |

*At serving time:* Deadhead the dahlia blossoms when they start to shed their petals. Before transplanting, check out the TIPS on pages 75 and 99.

*Pictured on page 86.*

# Strawberry Compote

This mixture of pinks is breathtaking! The hot portulaca fairly sizzles next to the tough geraniums.

*Suggested serving:* 14-16" (35-40 cm) color bowl or patio pot

*Temperature:* part sun, sun; moderate to high heat

| Ingredients: | 14-16" (35-40 cm) |
|---|---|
| ✤ geraniums, zonal, mixed, pinks and roses | 3 |
| ✯ portulaca, fuschia | 3 |

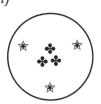

*At serving time:* Deadhead as needed. Do not over water!


# Flakes of Salmon

This arrangement is simplicity itself, but that doesn't stop it from being an eye-catcher! The phlox and alyssum trim the edge like icing on a cake, and the geranium keeps its spot as the centerpiece.

*Suggested serving:* 14-16" (35-40 cm) color bowl or patio pot

*Temperature:* shade, part sun, sun; low to high heat

| Ingredients: | 14-16" (35-40 cm) |
|---|---|
| ✤ geranium, zonal, salmon or white | 1 |
| ✯ phlox, Chanal | 3 |
| ★ alyssum, white | 3 |

*At serving time:* Deadhead as needed. See the TIP on page 73 about alyssum.

# Mellow Yellow

A dash of purple alyssum is added to the delicate buttery yellow petunias and marigolds. This dish looks good in any pot and really dresses up a dark container or wall.

*Suggested serving:* 14-16" (35-40 cm) color bowl or patio pot

*Temperature:* shade, part sun, sun; moderate heat

| *Ingredients:* | *14-16" (35-40 cm)* |
|---|---|
| ✤ petunia, single, yellow | 1 |
| ✱ marigolds, Sweet Cream | 2 |
| ☆ alyssum, purple | 4 |

*At serving time:* Deadhead as needed. See the TIP on page 73.

### TIP . . .

Toward the middle of August, **Sweet Cream** needs to be deadheaded whether you want to or not. After that, they'll keep right on blossoming till frost.

# Great Balls of Fire!

This pot sizzles with color and loves to bake in the hot sun! It's quick to assemble with only two items on the menu – fiery marigolds and showy verbena.

*Suggested serving:* 14-16" (35-40 cm) color bowl or patio pot

*Temperature:* shade, part sun, sun; moderate to high heat

| *Ingredients:* | *14-16" (35-40 cm)* |
|---|---|
| ✤ marigolds, orange or yellow, 8-12" (20-30 cm) | 5 |
| ✱ verbena, red, burgundy or purple | 5 |

*At serving time:* Deadhead as desired.

*Pictured on the back cover.*

# Sunny Boy

Everlastings are just that – everlasting; and that's helichrysum's pet name. Another name for it is strawflower. Both indicate that this flower is born dry so it can be kept eternally. Of course none of its titles suggest the bright colors they like to splash around! It blooms in an array of colors: yellow, red, orange, purple and burgundy. It holds its head up high among the alyssum and the daisies.

*Suggested serving:* 14-16" (35-40 cm) color bowl or patio pot

*Temperature:* part sun, sun; moderate to high heat

*Ingredients:*                    *14-16" (35-40 cm)*

| | |
|---|---|
| ❖ helichrysum, any color, | 1 |
|     12-14" (30-35 cm | |
| ✳ brachycome, mixed | 3 |
| ★ alyssum, purple | 3 |

*At serving time:* Deadhead the strawflowers. Trim the alyssum; see TIP on page 73, and trim the brachycome as needed. Keep on the dry side.

## TIP ...

To save your **everlastings**, add wire stems and make a long-lasting winter bouquet.

*Pictured on page 52.*

# Cotton Candy

If only it were edible! This little serving of creamy white, mauvy blue and bright orange looks delectable.

*Suggested serving:* 14-16" (35-40 cm) color bowl or patio pot

*Temperature:* shade, part sun, sun; low to moderate heat

· · · · · · · · · · · · · · · · · · · · · · · · · · · · · · · · · · · · · · · · · · · · · · · · · · · · · · · · · · · · · · · ·

| *Ingredients:* | *14-16" (35-40 cm)* |
|---|---|
| ❖ nemesia, white or mixed | 1 |
| ✩ ageratum, 8" (20 cm) | 4 |
| ★ zinnia, Classic Orange | 4 |

*At serving time:* Deadhead as desired.

**Variation:** Use **Crystal White zinnia** instead of the **Classic Orange**, for a softer look.

# Fruit and Dumplings

A short mixture that does well in pots that are on the shallow side, this combination is eye-catching and very different with the dainty clouds of green grass. I know, we certainly have our share of grass here in Saskatchewan, and our share of quack grass; so why would anyone want grass in a patio pot for goodness sake? Well, for myself, it reminds me of when I lived on the farm as a little girl and thought things like foxtail and buttercups and, yes, quack grass were beautiful, especially first thing in the morning, glistening with dew. And once you see it, you'll have to admit that this pot has an exotic appeal.

*Suggested serving:* 16" (40 cm) color bowl

*Temperature:* part sun, sun; moderate heat

*Ingredients:*                     *16" (40 cm)*

✤ grass, briza minor              1
✶ petunias, Fantasy Carmine       3
★ marigolds, yellow or gold,      3
    12" (30 cm)

*At serving time:* Deadhead as desired.

**TIP . . .**

Keep well fertilized. Don't let the pot dry out to the wilting point or the **grass** will turn yellow. Once the grass has bloomed – little round seed heads that seem to float over the rest of the pot – it must be deadheaded to keep it green longer. Near the end of the season it will turn completely yellow, no matter what you do, so at that point you might want to cut out the grass.

# Peach Cobbler

The shape of the pot inspires a different kind of casserole, loaded with color and full of texture. Geraniums know how to take the heat but let the alyssum and petunias take the space they need. The salmon, purple and white colors of this pot are always a classic combination.

*Suggested serving:* Approximately 16 x 20", (40 x 50 cm) oval or rectangular pot. These measurements were taken at the widest and longest parts of the pot.

*Temperature:* shade, part sun, sun; moderate heat

* * * * * * * * * * * * * * * * * * * * * * * * * * * * * * * * * * * * * * * * * * * * * * * * * * * * *

*Ingredients:*                    *16 x 20" (40 x 50 cm)*

♣ geranium, zonal, coral or          1
   dark salmon
✳ geraniums, zonal, salmon          2
   or light salmon
★ petunias, Fantasy Midnight        2
✳ alyssum, white                    2
✦ zinnias, Crystal White            2
   (optional)

*At serving time:* Deadhead as needed; see the TIP on page _73. Do not over-water.

**Variation:** For a change, or for those that prefer to stay away from petunias, try **neirembergia Purple Splendor** rather than the **Fantasy Midnight petunias.**

*Pictured on the front cover.*

# Jungle Basket

The begonias cook up some heat in any type of shade; the ivy creeps out of its container and escapes down the sides. The lobelia and the impatiens finish off the show with color and pizazz .

*Suggested serving:* 16 x 20" (40 x 50 cm) oval pot or smaller rectangular pot

*Temperature:* part sun, shade; low to moderate heat

- - - - - - - - - - - - - - - - - - - - - - - - - - - - - - - - - - - - - - - - - - - - - - - - - - - - - - - - - - - - -

| *Ingredients:* | *16 x 20" (40 x 50 cm)* |
|---|---|
| ❖ begonias, mixed colors | 2 |
| ✳ impatiens, mixed | 4 |
| ★ Kenilworth ivy (cymbalaria muralis) | 2 |
| ✳ lobelia, trailing, sapphire | 2 |

*At serving time:* Deadhead as desired. See the TIP on page 71. Refresh your memory on begonias with the TIPS on pages 82, 89 and 97.

*Pictured on page 119.*

# Dream Square

The little ferny leafed marigolds are a real contrast to the large open blossoms of the petunia. The pansies perk up the corners of the pot with rich color.

*Suggested serving:* 12-14" (30-35 cm) square pot

*Temperature:* shade, part sun, sun; low to moderate heat

- - - - - - - - - - - - - - - - - - - - - - - - - - - - - - - - - - - - - - - - - - - - - - - - - - - - - - - - - - - - -

| *Ingredients:* | *12-14" (30-35 cm)* |
|---|---|
| ❖ petunia, single, red | 1 |
| ✳ marigolds, signet yellow or gold | 2 |
| ★ pansies, mixed | 4 |

*At serving time:* See the TIP on page 75 about pansies. Deadhead as desired.

# Saucy Snaps

This snapdragon makes a great centerpiece, bushing out to fill the space. The rich petunias contrast well with the light blue lobelia and the baby snaps repeat the central theme.

*Suggested serving:* 12-16" (30-40 cm) square pot

*Temperature:* shade, part sun, sun; low to moderate heat

. . . . . . . . . . . . . . . . . . . . . . . . . . . . . . . . . . . . . . . . . . . . . . . . . . . . . . . . . . . . . . . . . . . .

*Ingredients:*                          *12-16" (30-40 cm)*

| | |
|---|---|
| ✤ snapdragon, 16-22" (40-55 cm) | 1 |
| ✲ petunias, single, burgundy | 2 |
| ★ lobelia, trailing, sky blue | 2 |
| ✳ snapdragons, 8" (20 cm) | 2 |

*At serving time:* Deadhead as desired. See the TIPS on page 71, 99 and 125.


# Layered Sunrise

Just picture the colorful sunrise of a prairie sky – this pot is what you might see. The bold yellows of the marigolds and daisies contrast with the majestic purple pansies and petunias.

*Suggested serving:* 14-16" (35-40 cm) square pot

*Temperature:* shade, part sun, sun; moderate heat

# Layered Sunrise continued

* * * * * * * * * * * * * * * * * * * * * * * * * * * * * * * * * * * * * * * * * * * * * * * * *

*Ingredients:*                                  *14-16" (35-40 cm)*

| | |
|---|---|
| ✤ marigold, yellow, 14-18" (35-45 cm) | 1 |
| ✳ petunias, Fantasy Midnight | 2 |
| ★ marigold, signet | 2 |
| ✱ Dahlberg daisy, Golden Fleece | 2 |
| ❊ pansies, Baby Bingo, Beaconsfield | 2 |

```
┌─────────────────┐
│ ✱    ☆    ✳      │
│                 │
│   ★   ♣   ★      │
│                 │
│ ✱    ☆    ✱      │
└─────────────────┘
```

*At serving time:* Deadhead as required. Refer to the TIP on page 75 for transplanting pansies.

# Breezy Soufflé

The dark purple neirembergia, with its fine-textured foliage, shine like little stars around the dark red petunia. The grass can be added for a fun and exotic touch, but the show can go on without it.

*Suggested Serving:* 26-32" (65-80 cm) by approximately
8-10" (20-25 cm) wide rectangular planter

*Temperature:* shade, part sun, sun; moderate heat

* * * * * * * * * * * * * * * * * * * * * * * * * * * * * * * * * * * * * * * * * * * * * * * * *

*Ingredients:*                         *26-32" x 8-10"*
                              *(65-80 cm) x (20-25 cm)*

| | |
|---|---|
| ✤ petunias, single red | 2 |
| ✳ neirembergia, Purple Splendor | 3 |
| ✦ grass, briza minor (optional) | 1 |

```
┌───────────────────────────────┐
│     ♣      ✦      ♣            │
│                               │
│  ☆         ☆           ☆       │
└───────────────────────────────┘
```

*At serving time:* Deadhead as needed. If you use the grass, see the TIP on page 109.

# Pink Impressions

It's the dianthus that shines here. This particular strain has flowers that come out white and turn pastel pink in youth, then deep ink as they mature. The alyssum provides an accent and the snaps a backdrop.

*Suggested serving:* 26-32" (66-80 cm) by 8-10" (20-25 cm) wide
rectangular planter

*Temperature:* shade, part sun, sun; low to moderate heat

| *Ingredients:* | *26-32" x 8-10"* |
| --- | --- |
| | *(65-80 cm x 20-25 cm)* |
| ❖ snapdragons, 12-14" (30-35 cm) high, mixed | 3 |
| ✳ dianthus, Diamond Blush Pink | 2 |
| ★ alyssum, rose or white | 2 |

*At serving time:* See the TIP on page 76 for deadheading dianthus. Trim alyssum according to the TIP on page 73 if necessary. Deadhead the snapdragons to keep them blooming. See the TIPS on pages 99 and 125.


# Bubble Burst

The yellow pansy just bursts in between the two layers of purple petunias and neirembergia, adding citrus spice.

*Suggested serving:* 26-32" (66-80 cm) by approximately
8-10" (20-25 cm) wide rectangular planter

*Temperature:* shade, part sun, sun; moderate heat

# Bubble Burst   continued

*Ingredients:*

26-32" x 8-10"
*(65-80 cm x 20-25 cm)*

| | |
|---|---|
| ✤ petunia, single, Midnight | 1 |
| ✷ pansy, yellow | 2 |
| ★ neirembergia, Purple Splendor | 4 |

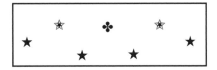

*At serving time:* Check the TIP on page 75 for planting instructions for the pansies. Deadhead as desired.


# Lemon Layered Aspic

The stark red and the blast of yellow line up on both sides of the frosty dusty miller, swirling with color.

*Suggested serving:* 28-34" (70-80 cm) by
8-10" (20-25 cm) wide rectangular planter

*Temperature:* shade, part sun, sun; low to moderate heat

*Ingredients:*

28-34" x 8-10"
*(70-80 cm x 20-25 cm)*

| | |
|---|---|
| ✤ nicotiana, red, 14-18" (35-45 cm) | 3 |
| ✷ dusty miller | 2 |
| ★ pansies, yellow | 3 |

*At serving time:* See the TIP on page 75 before transplanting the pansies. Deadhead as desired.

115

# Pink and Pretty Medley

The puffs of pink baby's breath fluff around the contrasting burgundy and orchid petunias, creating a soft and winsome beauty, easy to fall for.

*Suggested serving:* 28-34" (65-80 cm) by
                              8-10" (20-25 cm) rectangular planter

*Temperature:* shade, part sun, sun; moderate to high heat

· · · · · · · · · · · · · · · · · · · · · · · · · · · · · · · · · · · · · · · · · · · · · · · · · · · · · ·

| *Ingredients:* | *28-34" x 8-10"* |
| --- | --- |
| | *(70-80 cm x 20-25 cm)* |
| ❖ petunia, single, burgundy | 1 |
| ✳ petunia, single, orchid | 2 |
| ★ gypsophila, (baby's breath), | 2 |
|    Bridal Veil or Gypsy | |

*At serving time:* Deadhead as desired.

**TIP ...**
**If this pot will be seen from both sides**, line up the **baby's breath** with the **petunias**. If not, put them in slightly forward in the pot, as illustrated.

# Zesty Bouquet

This combination has the same color scheme as Sunny Delight below, but in this version the yellow daisies give a spicy contrast to the dianthus.

*Suggested serving:* 10-12" (25-30 cm) patio pot

*Temperature:* part sun, sun; low to moderate heat

*Ingredients:*                         *10-12" (25-30 cm)*

❖ dianthus, any vibrant color     3
✳ Dahlberg daisies, Golden        3
   Fleece

*At serving time:* Deadhead as desired; check out the TIP on page 76.

# Sunny Delight

Though the Multicaule is not well-known, it's worth finding to have its sunny yellow buttercup blossoms peeking through the dianthus. The marbled effect it creates is wonderful.

*Suggested serving:* 10-12" (30-35 cm) patio pot

*Temperature:* part sun, sun; low to moderate heat

*Ingredients:*                         *10-12" (30-35 cm)*

❖ chrysanthemum, Multicaule      1
✳ dianthus, any vibrant color     3

*At serving time:* The multicaule looks much better deadheaded; it's a small effort that makes a difference; see the TIP on page 76.

# Pot of Gold

All yellow, this pot sizzles in any corner! The pompon marigold and the flat-faced pansies are surrounded by a sprinkle of breezy daisies.

*Suggested serving:* 10-16" (30-35 cm) upright pot

*Temperature:* part sun, sun; moderate heat

| Ingredients: | 10"<br>(25 cm) | 12-14"<br>(30-35 cm) | 16"<br>(40 cm) |
|---|---|---|---|
| ✤ marigold, yellow<br>    14-18" (35-45 cm) | 1 | 1 | 3 |
| ✹ pansies, clear yellow | 2 | 3 | 4 |
| ★ Dahlberg daisies,<br>    Golden Fleece | 2 | 3 | 4 |

*At serving time:* Deadhead as needed. See the TIP on page 75 before planting in the pansies.

*Pictured on page 86.*

1   *Dream Drop, page 82*
2   *Fancy Pansy, page 91*
3   *Soupe du Jour, page 146*
4   *Crystallized Sunshine, page 137*
5   *Summer Essence, page 143*
6   *Jungle Basket, page 111*
7   *Ambrosia, page 101*
8   *Herb Dip with Veggies, page 142*

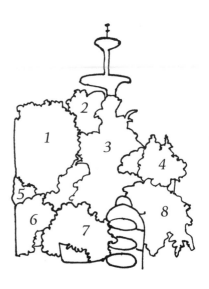

# Glazed Crunch

The sunshiny Lunette beams around the red petunias. The sprinkling of viola adds texture and interest with both its blossoms and leaves.

*Suggested serving:* 10-16" (25-40 cm) patio pot

*Temperature:* part sun, sun; moderate to high heat

| *Ingredients:* | 10-12"<br>(25-30 cm) | 14-16"<br>(35-40 cm) |
|---|---|---|
| ❖ petunias, single, red | 2 | 3 |
| ✳ mesembryanthemum, Lunette | 2 | 3 |
| ★ violas, mixed | 2 | 3 |

*At serving time:* Deadhead the Lunette; deadhead the rest as needed or desired; see the TIP on page 75 for pansy or viola planting instructions.

*Pictured on the front cover.*

## TIP . . .

**Mesembryanthemum** is just as pretty by any other name – **Iceplant**, **Livingstone Daisy** or, in the case of one particular yellow, **Lunette** (it's special because it has a bright rosy-red center). This is why it's important to know the **latin name** of some plants – they can have so many common names as to be confusing, or one or more of the common names may also apply to other plants! Knowing the Latin name simplifies finding it in seed catalogues and gardening books.

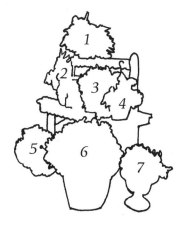

# Fruit Cake

The rich color of the dianthus is defined by charming white mums and blue pompom ageratums.

*Suggested serving:* 10-16" (25-40 cm) patio pot

*Temperature:* shade, part sun, sun; low to moderate heat

| *Ingredients:* | 10-12"<br>(25-30 cm) | 14-16"<br>(35-40 cm) |
|---|---|---|
| ✤ dianthus, any color | 1 | 3 |
| ✶ maticaria, Santana | 2 | 3 |
| ★ ageratum, 8-10" (20-25 cm) blue | 2 | 3 |

*At serving time:* See the TIP about dianthus on page 76. Deadhead as desired.

**Variation:** If you like to keep it simple, in the 10-12" (25-30 cm) range of pots, you can put in **3 Santana** rather than **2 Santana** and **2 ageratum**.

*Pictured on the back cover.*


# Éclair

Beautiful in its simplicity, this pot is composed of only two colors: bright yellow and cool blue. But there's more than a pinch of texture here with the ferny leaf of the delicate daisy, the broad green strokes of the pansy leaves, the marigold pompoms, not to mention the perky pansy faces.

*Suggested serving:* 10-18" (30-45 cm) patio pot

*Temperature:* shade, part sun, sun; low to moderate heat

| Ingredients: | 10"<br>(25 cm) | 12-14"<br>(30-35 cm) | 16-18"<br>(40-45 cm) |
|---|---|---|---|
| ❖ marigold, any color,<br>  14-18" (35-45 cm) | 1 | 1 | 3 |
| ✭ pansies, blue | 2 | 3 | 3 |
| ★ Dahlberg daisies,<br>  Golden Fleece | 2 | 3 | 3 |

*At serving time:* See TIP on page 75 before planting pansies. Deadhead as desired.

**Variation:** Add a **dracaena spike** to the center of the large pots (16-18" [41-45 cm]) to add height and interest; or try a taller **marigold** in the center, say an 18-24" (45-60 cm) high **Lady** or **Jubilee**.

*Pictured on page 33.*

# Rose Splash

The old-fashioned schizanthus makes a comeback in this saucy pot! Its florets look like miniature orchids, it's nickname "poor man's orchid". Combined with dianthus and lobelia it makes a flourish of color and texture.

*Suggested serving:* 12-16" (30-40 cm) patio pot
*Temperature:* shade, part sun, sun; low to moderate heat

| Ingredients: | 12-14"<br>(30-35 cm) | 16"<br>(40 cm) |
|---|---|---|
| ❖ schizanthus, any color | 1 | 3 |
| ✭ dianthus, rose | 2 | 3 |
| ✳ lobelia, trailing, rose | 2 | 3 |
| ★ lobelia, upright, rose | 2 | 3 |

*At serving time:* Deadhead as needed. Trim lobelia if scraggly, see TIP on page 71; check out dianthus TIP on page 76 and the schizanthus tip on page 101.

*Pictured on page 120.*

# Wild Africa

The large daisy in the center sprawls all over the place, like a wild jungle animal but, though it looks wild and exotic, it doesn't take over. There's plenty of contrast, both in color and foliage – not for the faint of heart!

*Suggested serving:* 12-16" (30-40 cm) patio pot

*Temperature:* part sun, sun; moderate to high heat

*Ingredients:*               *12-16" (30-40 mL)*

♣ **dimorphotheca (African Daisy)**      1
✴ **chrysanthemum, Snowland**      3

*At serving time:* Deadhead as needed; both will stop blooming if allowed to go to seed. See the TIP on page 121 about common names.


# Oeux à la Neige

These coquettish daisies don't need any help! They put on their own show with color and texture built into the plant!

*Suggested serving:* 12-16" (30-40 cm) patio pot

*Temperature:* part sun, sun; moderate heat

*Ingredients:*               *12-16" (30-40 cm)*

♣ **chrysanthemum, Snowland**      3

*At serving time:* Deadhead occasionally; Snowland will go to seed and stop blooming if left completely to its own devices. Pick a bouquet every once in a while – after all we are talking chrysanthemums and all chrysanthemums make good cut flowers.

*Pictured on page 34.*

# Shy Show

Though the colors are bright and the texture interesting, this ensemble is a simple design. The sunny marigolds are enhanced by the color of the snap-dragons. The shy Livingstone Daisy (mesembryanthemum), opening fully in daylight, gives this pot a whimsical quality.

*Suggested serving:* 12-16" (30-40 cm) patio pot

*Temperature:* part shade, part sun, sun; moderate to high heat

| Ingredients: | 12-14"<br>(30-35 cm) | 16"<br>(40 cm) |
| --- | --- | --- |
| ❖ marigold, yellow or gold, 14-18"<br>(35-45 cm) | 1 | 1 |
| ✳ petunias, rose or carmine | 2 | 3 |
| ★ snapdragons, mixed, 8" (20 cm) | 2 | 2 |
| ✴ mesembryanthemum, mix | 2 | 2 |

*At serving time:* Deadhead the Livingstone Daisy as needed; other plants as desired. See the TIP on page 121 about mesembryanthemum, and TIP on pages 99 about snapdragons.

## Tip . . .

To deadhead the composite flowers of the **snapdragons**, wait until almost all of the florets have finished blooming, then cut off that branch to the base.

*Pictured on page 85.*

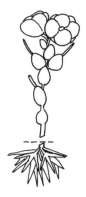

# Paisley Patchwork

The African Daisy swirls through and around the red dianthus and purple alyssum; the sunny yellow Lunette (mesembryanthemum) gives contrast.

*Suggested serving:* 12-16" (30-40 cm) patio pot

*Temperature:* part sun, sun; moderate heat

| *Ingredients:* | *12-14"* (30-35 cm) | *16"* (40 cm) |
|---|---|---|
| ✤ dimorphotheca, African Daisy | 1 | 1 |
| ✳ dianthus, red | 3 | 3 |
| ★ alyssum, purple | 2 | 3 |
| ✱ mesembryanthemum, Lunette (or any yellow available) | 2 | 3 |

*At serving time:* Deadhead the daisies as needed. See the TIPS on pages 76 and 73 for deadheading dianthus and alyssum. Also see he TIP on latin names on page 121.

*Pictured on page 120.*

# Piquante Daisy

The white daisy-like Snowland has a yellow center that brightens up the pot. The pompom marigolds contrast well with the dark and dainty lobelia. All in all, it's a class act.

*Suggested serving:* 12-16" (30-35 cm) patio pot

*Temperature:* shade, part sun, sun; moderate heat

# Piquante Daisy    continued

| Ingredients: | 12-14" (30-35 cm) | 16" (40 cm) |
| --- | --- | --- |
| ✤ chrysanthemum, Snowland | 1 | 2 |
| ✩ marigold, 10-12" (25-30 cm) (Disco queen is pictured) | 2 | 3 |
| ★ lobelia, upright, Crystal Palace | 2 | 3 |

*At serving time:* Deadhead as needed. To trim lobelia, see the TIP on page 71.

*Pictured on page 51.*

# Muffin Head

Petunias and pansies are a bright, cheerful and classy combination that mound over the edge of the pot. Adorable!

*Suggested serving:* 12-16" (30-40 cm) patio pot
*Temperature:* shade, part sun, sun; moderate heat

| Ingredients: | 12-14" (30-35 cm) | 16" (40 cm) |
| --- | --- | --- |
| ✤ petunias, single, burgundy or rose or carmine | 3 | 4 |
| ✩ pansies, clear yellow | 3 | 3 |

*At serving time:* Deadhead as needed. Check out the TIP on page 75 for instructions on pansies.

**Variation:** Substitute a **dracaena spike** for the center **petunia** in the 16" (40 cm) pot. If it's your style, in the 12-14" (30-35 cm) pot, also add a spike in the center, leaving everything else as sketched.

*Pictured on page 51.*

127

# Cream Puff

This light and airy concoction is like a cloud of pastels accented with color –
the pastel pink of the baby's breath with the deep purple of the nierembergia. The white geranium ties it all together with its rose eye.

*Suggested serving:* 12-16" (25-40 cm) patio pot

*Temperature:* shade, part sun, sun; moderate to high heat

· · · · · · · · · · · · · · · · · · · · · · · · · · · · · · · · · · · · · · · · · · · · · · · · · · · · · · · · · · · · · · · · · · ·

*Ingredients:*           *12-16" (25-40 cm)*

❖ **geranium, zonal, white with**     1
   **a rose or pink eye, or rose**
✴ **gypsophila, Bridal Veil**     2
   **or Gypsy**
★ **nierembergia, Purple**     2
   **Splendor**

*At serving time:* Deadhead as desired; be sure not to let the flowers wilt as the
gypsophila will not recover very well.

**TIP . . .**
What's an eye, you say? It's a little splash of color on each petal, near the heart
of the flower.


# Summer Riches

Another class act – the begonias just can't help it – with large buttery yellow
blossoms and purple pansy finery. The Super Elfin, on the side, is always at
its best.

*Suggested serving:* 12-18" (30-45 cm) patio pot

*Temperature:* shade, part sun; low to moderate heat

| Ingredients: | 12-14" (30-35 cm) | 16-18" (40-45 cm) |
|---|---|---|
| ❖ begonias, Non-Stop, yellow | 2 | 3 |
| ✵ impatiens, Super Elfin, raspberry | 2 | 3 |
| ★ pansy, Purple Rain | 2 | 3 |
| ✦ dracaena spike (optional) | 2 | 3 |

*At serving time:* See the TIP on page 75 for pansy planting. Keep the pansies under control by trimming as needed. See the TIPS on pages 82, 89 and 97 about begonias. Deadhead as needed. See the TIP on page 71 about impatiens.

*Pictured on page 51.*


# Party Punch

It's true, the nicotiana does give a punch of color. Not only does it have star-like blooms, it also attracts butterflies and hummingbirds with its color and scent. The brachycome surrounds it with a spray of mauve and purple daisies.

*Suggested serving:* 12-18" (30-45 cm) patio pot

*Temperature:* part sun, sun; moderate to high heat

| Ingredients: | 12-14" (30-35 cm) | 16-18" (40-45 cm) |
|---|---|---|
| ❖ nicotiana, any color, 12-16" (30-40 cm) | 1 | 3 |
| ✵ brachycome, mixed | 4 | 6 |

*At serving time:* Deadhead as desired.

*Pictured on page 86.*

# Tangy Fiesta

The brilliant magenta of the carmine, or the rose if you choose, is lightened by the silver of the dusty miller and the gold of the little dahlberg daisies. The puffs of ageratum finish off the show.

*Suggested serving:* 12-18" (30-45 cm) patio pot

*Temperature:* part sun, sun; moderate to high heat

| Ingredients: | 12-14" (30-35 cm) | 16-18" (60-45 cm) |
|---|---|---|
| ❖ petunias, single carmine or rose | 2 | 3 |
| ✭ dusty miller, Cirrus | 2 | 3 |
| ★ Dahlberg daisies, Golden Fleece | 2 | 3 |
| ✳ ageratum, 8-10" (20-25 cm), blue | 2 | 3 |

*At serving time:* Deadhead occasionally or as needed.

**Variation:** Use **dusty miller Silver Dust** rather than **Cirrus** if you like. What I like about Cirrus is that it is so vigorous; it keeps its frosty color all season long and has great rain and frost tolerance.
*Pictured on the front cover.*

# Autumn Treat

The asters bloom last, but even before flowering, the plants give the pot texture and contrast, with their broad-cut leaves. Blooming last but longer, expect the asters to give color well into the fall. And, you can use them as short, cut flowers to adorn your kitchen table!

*Suggested serving:* 12-18" (40-45 cm) patio pot

*Temperature:* part sun, sun; moderate to high heat

| Ingredients: | 12-14"<br>(30-35 cm) | 16-18"<br>(40-45 cm) |
|---|---|---|
| ✤ petunia, single, purple | 1 | 1 |
| ✳ asters, mixed, 8-12" (20-30 cm) high | 2 | 3 |
| ★ mesembryanthemum, mixed | 2 | 3 |
| ✱ alyssum, white | 2 | 3 |

*At serving time:* See the names TIP, page 121; see alyssum TIP, page 73.


# Tutti Frutti

The double pink rosettes of the phlox are a perfect contrast to the large creamy blooms of the marigold; mind you, both are soft in color and make good use of the plum purple accent of the alyssum.

*Suggested serving:* 12-22" (30-55 cm)patio pot

*Temperature:* part sun, sun; hot to moderate heat, shade

| Ingredients: | 12"<br>(30 cm) | 14-16"<br>(35-40 cm) | 18-22"<br>(45-55 cm) |
|---|---|---|---|
| ✤ marigolds,<br>    Sweet Cream | 1 | 1 | 3 |
| ✳ phlox, Chanal | 3 | 4 | 5 |
| ★ alyssum, purple | 3 | 4 | 5 |

*At serving time:* Deadhead as desired. Trim alyssum if it shows signs of going to seed. See the TIPS on pages 73 and 106.

*Pictured on page 86.*

# Summer Extravagance

This heavenly confection is a focal point wherever it is served. It really does look good enough to eat! The vibrant violet geranium is lit up by the bright yellow begonias. What makes this arrangement so outstanding is the combination of these two classics. Of course, the clouds of lilac lobela and the Creeping Jenny cascading to the ground doesn't hurt either!

*Suggested serving:* 14-16" (35-40 cm) patio pot,
   preferably on a stand or pedestal

*Temperature:* shade, part sun; low to moderate heat

- - - - - - - - - - - - - - - - - - - - - - - - - - - - - - - - - - - - - - - - - - - - - - - - - - -

*Ingredients:* 　　　　　　　　　　*14-16" (35-40 cm)*

| | |
|---|---|
| ✤ geraniums, zonal, grape or violet | 2 |
| ✯ begonias, Non-Stop, yellow | 2 |
| ★ Creeping Jenny, (lysimachia nummularia) | 2 |
| ✳ lobelia, trailing, lilac | 2 |
| ✦ dracaena spike (*optional*) | 1 |

*At serving time:* Deadhead as desired. See the TIP on page 71 for information on trimming lobelia if it gets scraggly. See the TIPS on pages 82, 89 and 97 on growing and deadheading begonias.

*Pictured on page 33.*

# Fricassée

Bright, bold and yes, beautiful! You can always count on dianthus to attract attention, especially when they are teamed up with yellow – pansies in this case. The lobelia spills over the edge, softening the arrangement.

*Suggested serving:* 14-16" (35-40 cm) patio pot

*Temperature:* shade, part sun, sun; low to moderate heat

# Fricassée continued

*Ingredients:*          14-16" *(35-40 cm)*

| | |
|---|---|
| ♣ dianthus, crimson, red, violet, purple or rose | 3 |
| ✻ pansies, clear yellow | 3 |
| ★ lobelia, trailing, sapphire | 3 |

*At serving time:* To get it right the first time see the TIP on page 75 about transplanting pansies. See TIPS on pages 71 and 76 about dead-heading.

*Pictured on page 85.*

# Heaven Scent

Heliotrope is not called Vanilla plant for nothing! Set this plant near any entrance and get a whiff of it every time you go by. Let's not forget that petunias smell nice too – especially the dark purple. These two species, along with the alyssum, ensure a scent of heaven

*Suggested serving:* 14-16" (35-40 cm) patio pot

*Temperature:* part sun, sun; moderate to high heat

*Ingredients:*          14-16" *(35-40 cm)*

| | |
|---|---|
| ♣ heliotrope | 1 |
| ✻ petunias, single pink or salmon, veined or solid | 3 |
| ★ petunias, Fantasy Midnight | 2 |
| ✳ alyssum, white | 2 |

*At serving time:* Deadhead as desired. Trim alyssum if it begins to go to seed, following the TIP on page 73.

## TIP . . .

Pinch off the center of the **heliotrope** once or twice, to get it to bush out more. Do this at the very start of the season and you will have a lovely plant. By the way, you may end up having to stake it.

*Pictured on page 52.*

133

# Dash of Flash

Although the other ingredients could stand on their own, the grass in the center of the pot adds a focal point as well as fill. Its seed heads sway over the dianthus and violas. With the bright version of the old-fashioned "pinks" (dianthus) and the sweet violas, who needs anything more?

*Suggested serving:* 14-16" (35-40 cm) patio pot

*Temperature:* part sun, sun; moderate heat

· · · · · · · · · · · · · · · · · · · · · · · · · · · · · · · · · · · · · · · · · · · · · · · · · · · · · ·

*Ingredients:*                    *14-16" (35-40 cm)*

✤ dianthus, any color          3
✲ violas, mixed                 3
✦ grass, briza maxima (*optional*)  1

*At serving time:* Deadhead as desired. See TIPS on pages 75 and 76 for transplanting and deadheading violas and dianthus.

**TIP . . .**
**Briza Maxima** is a close relative of the **Briza Minor**, but it's tougher and lives longer. Simply deadhead it occasionally and it will keep doing its job.

# Spiced Chiffon

The creamy marigold pops up over the dark burgundy; the delicate diascia weaves in and out and all around.

*Suggested serving:* 14-16" (35-40 cm) patio pot

*Temperature:* shade, part sun, sun; moderate to high heat

# Spiced Chiffon   continued

*Ingredients:*                     *14-16" (35-40 cm)*

♣ marigold, Sweet Cream          1
✿ petunias, single or double,    3
    burgundy
★ diascia                        3

*At serving time:* Deadhead as desired. See the TIP on page 106 for more information on the Sweet Cream.

*Pictured on the front cover.*


# Razzle Dazzle

The color combination of the carmine and lilac is both bold and bashful. The alyssum and the violas peek around the edge, complimenting the petunias.

*Suggested serving:* 14-16" (35-40 cm) patio pot

*Temperature:* shade, part sun, sun; moderate heat

*Ingredients:*                     *14-16" (35-40 cm)*

♣ petunias, single, carmine      2
✿ petunias, single, lilac        2
★ viola, mixed                   2
✳ alyssum, white or rose         2

*At serving time:* See the TIP on page 75 for planting violas and the TIP on page 73 about deadheading alyssum.

135

# Peach Melba

If you love geraniums as I do – you'll go for this combo. Geraniums have a long history in this part of the country; I think it was the only flowering plant true farmers were allowed to have. It seems almost all houses had a few dried up geraniums trying to winter on a frosty window sill, filling the air with their distinctive scent (or smell, depending on whether or not you like it). This gave all geraniums a bad name. I have to admit, when I first got into plants, geraniums were not my bag, but now, after a few years of experience and experiments, I appreciate their value.

As for violas, there is a wild strain that grows here – a very dainty little violet. The tamed version has lovely color that pulses around the geraniums and the petunias in this container.

*Suggested serving:* 14-16" (35-40 cm) patio pot

*Temperature:* shade, part sun, sun; low to high heat

· · · · · · · · · · · · · · · · · · · · · · · · · · · · · · · · · · · · · · · · · · · · · · · · · · · · · · · · · · · · · · · ·

*Ingredients:*         *14-16" (35-40 cm)*

| | |
|---|---|
| ❧ geraniums, zonal, salmon | 2 |
| ✴ petunias, Fantasy Crystal Red | 2 |
| ★ violas, mixed | 2 |

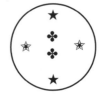

*At serving time:* Deadhead as desired. Read the TIP on page 75 before you put in the violas.

*Pictured on the back cover.*

# Color Buffet

This combo is a bright and vibrant dish – splashes of yellow break up the clouds of purple.

*Suggested serving:* 14-18" (35-45 cm) patio pot

*Temperature:* part sun, sun; moderate heat

*Ingredients:*            14-18" (35-45 cm)

✤ petunias, single, yellow          2
✾ petunias, Fantasy Midnight        2
★ neirembergia, Purple Splendor 2
✳ Dahlberg daisies, Golden          2
    Fleece

*At serving time:* Deadhead as desired.


# Crystallized Sunshine

This combo screams out summer and sunshine and lollipops and rainbows! The short Brown-Eyed Susans smile through the silver foliage of the dusty miller; the Victoria salvia adds a touch of height with it's contrasting purple.

*Suggested serving:* 14-18" (35-45 cm) patio pot

*Temperature:* shade, part sun, sun; moderate to high heat

| *Ingredients:* | 12" (30 cm) | 14-16" (35-40 cm) | 18" (45 cm) |
|---|---|---|---|
| ✤ salvia, Victoria | 1 | 1 | 3 |
| ✾ dusty miller, Cirrus | 2 | 3 | 3 |
| ★ rudbeckia (Brown-Eyed Susan), 6-12" (15-30 cm) | 2 | 3 | 3 |

*At serving time:* Deadhead as desired.

*Pictured on page 119.*

# Extravagance

Godetia is a little known, old-fashioned flower that sometime goes under the name "Satin flower". The "satin" comes from the sheen of the petals, which seem to have the color painted on with a brush. It has a palette that runs the gammit from rosy-red to pink to coral and mauve. Its most wonderful asset is that it will perform anywhere but thrives in absolute shade, where no other plant deigns to grow. If you have a deep and dank spot you need to liven up, and haven't had much luck so far, try Godetia. You won't regret it.

*Suggested serving:* 14-22" (45-55 cm) patio pot

*Temperature:* deep shade, shade, sun, part sun; low to moderate heat

| Ingredients: | 14-16"<br>(35-40 cm) | 18-22"<br>(45-55 cm) |
|---|---|---|
| ✤ petunias, rose or pink | 3 | 3 |
| ✸ godetia, mixed | 4 | 8 |

*At serving time:* Deadhead as needed.

**Variations:** Rather than **petunias**, try **geraniums** in the center for sunny to shady areas; try one **American Giant begonia** for part shade or shade; or use one lavatera plant for sun, part sun; moderate heat.

# Summer Surprise

Anybody that might think they'd seen everything haven't seen this container! Although different, this pot is an easily digestible feast for the eyes. The chard has a burgundy-green color and distinctive texture. The red petunias highlight the chard and the marigold and the daisies provide contrast.

*Suggested serving:* 16-18" (40-45 cm) patio pot

*Temperature:* sun, part sun; moderate to high heat

*Ingredients:*           *16-18" (40-45 cm)*

| | |
|---|---|
| ❖ Swiss chard, Bright Lights, red | 1 |
| ✳ petunias, single, red | 2 |
| ★ marigolds, Lulu | 2 |
| ✳ Dahlberg daisies, Golden Fleece | 2 |
| ✦ verbena, red (optional) | 2 |

*At serving time:* Deadhead occasionally; remove the outer leaves of the chard from time to time in order to give the rest of the plants a chance to perform.

## Tip ...

**Start your own chard from seed** about six weeks before you want it to go out – or even right in the pot. Put in three or four seeds about the same depth as the thickness of the seed. Once the plants are growing, choose the one with the darkest-colored leaf to use in your pot and cut out the rest.

*Pictured on the back cover.*

# Fire-Glow

Here's another floral and vegetable beauty. The Swiss chard stands majestically in the center, adding not only height, but visual appeal and contrast as well. The cheerful marigold put up a colorful show with the bold petunias. The Santana adds a dainty touch.

*Suggested serving:* 16-18" (40-45 cm) patio pot

*Temperature:* shade, part sun, sun; moderate to high heat

*Ingredients:*                     *16-18" (40-45 cm)*

| | |
|---|---|
| ❖ Swiss chard, Bright Lights, yellow | 1 |
| ✮ marigold, signet, Lulu | 2 |
| ★ marigolds, any color, 12" (30 cm) | 2 |
| ✳ petunias, Fantasy Red or Fantasy Midnight | 4 |
| ✲ matricaria, Santana or White stars | 2 |

*At serving time:* Deadhead as desired. Remove the outer leaves of the Swiss chard as it grows; see the TIP on page 139 for seeding the chard.

*Pictured on page 85.*

# Chiffon Ruffle

The round double blossom of the petunia is a good match for the large marigold bloom, and the colors provide delicate contrast. The ageratum and the Santana trim the edge.

*Suggested serving:* 18-20" (45-50 cm) patio pot

*Temperature:* shade, part sun, sun; high to moderate heat

| *Ingredients:* | *18-20" (45-50 cm)* |
|---|---|
| ❖ dracaena spike | 1 |
| ✴ marigold, Sweet Cream | 2 |
| ★ petunias, double, Cascade Series, any color | 2 |
| ✳ matricaria, Santana | 4 |
| ✲ ageratum, 8" (20 cm) | 4 |

*At serving time:* Deadhead as desired or as needed. See the TIP on page 106 about Sweet Cream.

*Variation:* Use **yellow marigolds** if you like, rather than the **off-white, Sweet Cream**.

*Pictured on page 52.*

# Herb Dip with Veggies

I got 14 tomatoes off the one plant when I made up this pot in my test kitchen. I might add that the whole pot was a favorite of family and friends! It's like a living salad with all kinds of interesting texture and great scent and, yes, even color – remember, tomatoes do bloom and cukes have little yellow blossoms. The marjoram and the thyme put in their twos scents worth with color too, if they're neglected long enough to bloom! Oh, yes – even the violas are edible!

*Suggested serving:* 18-20" (45-50 cm) patio pot

*Temperature:* sun, part sun; moderate to high heat

*Ingredients:*                                      *18-20" (45-50 cm)*

| | |
|---|---|
| ❖ Tomato, bush type (use a hybrid for best results) | 1 |
| ✫ cucumber, bush type | 1 |
| ★ dill plant, Fernleaf | 1 |
| ✳ parsley, Moss Curled | 1 |
| ✻ marjoram | 1 |
| ❖ thyme | 1 |
| ✦ violas, mixed (optional) | 2 |

*At serving time:* Fertilize regularly; water deeply, but allow to dry out in-between. Trim herbs as needed in the kitchen; eat tomatoes and cucumbers when ripe; enjoy.

**Variations:** Thyme comes in various flavors, scents and colors – try lemon thyme or apple or other varieties; **French thyme** has narrow leaves and **English thyme** has broad.

*Pictured on page 119.*

142

# Summer Essence

The depth of the purple offered by heliotrope is matched only by its perfume. The white and Burgundy Star petunia adds a festive air and the soft yellow petunia lightens up the whole arrangement.

*Suggested serving:* 18-20" (45-50 cm) patio pot

*Temperature:* part sun, sun; moderate to high heat

* * * * * * * * * * * * * * * * * * * * * * * * * * * * * * * * * * * * * * * * * * * * * * * * * * * *

*Ingredients:*　　　　　　　　*18-20" (45-50 cm)*

| | |
|---|---|
| ✤ heliotrope | 1 |
| ✵ petunias, single, Burgundy Star | 2 |
| ★ petunias, single, yellow | 2 |

*At serving time:* Deadhead as desired. For more on heliotrope see the TIP on page 133.


# Limòn Sorbet

If this pot were a cocktail it would surely be a margarita – it is so vivacious! Individual flowers and foliage are delicate, but the effect is tangy and tart.

*Suggested serving:* 18-22" (45-55 cm) patio pot

*Temperature:* part sun, shade; low to moderate heat

* * * * * * * * * * * * * * * * * * * * * * * * * * * * * * * * * * * * * * * * * * * * * * * * * * * *

*Ingredients:*　　　　　　　　*18-22" (45-55 cm)*

| | |
|---|---|
| ✤ begonia, white, red, orange, salmon or apricot | 1 |
| ✵ coleus, lime colored | 3 |
| ★ pansies, clear blue | 3 |
| ✳ nemesia, white or mixed | 3 |

*At serving time:* Before you start, see TIPS on pages 75, 82, 89 and 97. Deadhead as desired. Trim the coleus if it begins to take over.

*Pictured on the front cover.*

# Cherry Slices

Talk about bright! A mix of purple, red and yellow petunias are tied in a bow by the vinca vine.

*Suggested serving:* 18-20" (45-50 cm) patio pot

*Temperature:* part sun, sun, moderate to high heat

* * * * * * * * * * * * * * * * * * * * * * * * * * * * * * * * * * * * * * * * * * * * * * * * * * * * * * * * * * * * *

*Ingredients:*                          *18-20" (45-50 cm)*

❖ dracaena spike                  1
✶ petunias, single, purple      2
★ petunias, single, yellow      2
✳ petunias, single, red          3
✲ snapdragons, 8-10" (20-25 cm)  4
◆ vinca vine (optional)          1

*At serving time:* Deadhead as desired; see the TIPS on pages 125 and 96.

**TIP . . .**

Trim the **vinca vine** once, as illustrated to encourage it to bush out. The vine is optional. If you don't use it, place the fourth snapdragon in its spot.

# Daisy-a-Day

Scrumptious to behold, the Sonata White cosmos stands above the rest, blowing with the breeze along with the Snowland. The brick-red gaillardia provides colorful contrast to all the white flowers and silver foliage around it.

*Suggested serving:* 18-24" (45-50 cm) patio pot

*Temperature:* part sun, sun; moderate to high heat

| Ingredients: | 18-20" (45-50 cm) | 22-24" (55-60 cm) |
|---|---|---|
| ✣ cosmos, Sonata White | 1 | 1 |
| ✳ chrysanthemum, Snowland | 2 | 3 |
| ★ gaillardia, Red Plume | 2 | 3 |
| ✵ dusty miller, Cirrus | 2 | 3 |

*At serving time:* Deadhead as needed. Use any or all of these as cut flowers.

*Pictured on page 120.*

# Raving Wave

Say what you will about the Wave series of petunias – they certainly know how to perform – and with such easy care!

*Suggested serving:* 18-26" (45-65 cm) patio pot

*Temperature:* shade, part sun, sun; moderate to high heat

- - - - - - - - - - - - - - - - - - - - - - - - - - - - - - - - - - - - - - - - - - - - - - - - - - - - - - - -

*Ingredients:*                          *18-26" (45-65 cm)*

✤ petunias, Wave,              3
    pink, rose, lilac mist,
    or a mixture of all three;
    or purple, or coral

*At serving time:* Deadhead as desired or as needed. Waves only seem to need deadheading after a rainstorm – otherwise, they're really independent.

**Variation:** Put a large **dracaena spike** smack-dab in the middle of the pot.

**TIP ...**
Independent as they are, **Wave petunias** still like to be well-fed. Fertilize regularly.


# Soupe du Jour

This simmering of veggies and flora is to be savored by more than the sense of sight. The alyssum adds perfume; the corn and the geranium add texture; the tomato, taste; and if you use a miniature popcorn, it will add sound to the repertoire.

I should let you know that I got more tomatoes off that Tumbler tomato than I have ever seen on one plant. Though they are the size of a cherry tomato, they have a true garden tomato taste.

*Suggested serving:* 20-22" (50-55 cm) patio pot

*Temperature:* part sun, sun; moderate to high heat

# Soupe du Jour continued

. . . . . . . . . . . . . . . . . . . . . . . . . . . . . . . . . . . . . . . . . . . . . . . . . . .

*Ingredients:*                           *20-22" (50-55 cm)*

❖ baby corn (I used Cutie Blues)     1
✾ geraniums, Zonal, red              2
★ tomato, Tumbler                    1
✳ rudbeckia, 8-10" (20-25 cm)        4
✣ alyssum, purple                    2

*At serving time:* Fertilize heavily, water deeply. Deadhead geraniums as needed, allowing the top of the soil to dry out a bit between watering. See TIP on page 73 for trimming alyssum. Pig out on cherry tomatoes when ripe; have a feed of corn. See the seeding TIP on page 139 and use the chard seeding instructions for the corn, if you decide to go that route.

*Pictured on page 119.*

# Hawaiian Salad

Think tropical when you think begonias. After all that's where they originated. When you combine them with sprawling Imagination verbena, the profuse godetia and the tangle of ivy, you've got a jungle in your back yard!

*Suggested serving:* 20-22" (50-55 cm) patio pot

*Temperature:* part sun, shade; moderate heat

. . . . . . . . . . . . . . . . . . . . . . . . . . . . . . . . . . . . . . . . . . . . . . . . . . .

*Ingredients:*                           *20-22" (50-55 cm)*

❖ verbena, Imagination               1
✾ begonias, American Giant,          3
   all pink, salmon or apricot;
   may be pendulas or a mix
   of upright and pendulas
★ godetia, mixed                     3
✳ Kenilworth ivy (cymbalaria         3
   muralis)

*At serving time:* Deadhead as desired. Check out TIPS on pages 82, 89 and 97 for all the information you may need for begonias.

# Color Index

This index should be helpful for putting pots together following a color scheme, and also for finding individual pots. Hopefully, it will become a practical tool for you.

The pots are listed under their most predominant color, along with the most predominant accent color. This does not mean that there are no other colors in the container. The mixtures of colors are listed as such. That means that if you have as a predominant plant, helichrysum (strawflower), it will probably come from a mix and you can't predict the color, e.g., the recipe Sunny Boy, on page 107, is under "mixture". Sometimes, both the focus plant and the mass and fill are mixes as well; these are also listed under mixture.

# Share *The Joy of Gardening* with a friend

Order *The Joy of Gardening* at $14.95 per book plus $4.00 (total order) for postage and handling.

Number of books _____ x $14.95 = $ _____
Shipping and handling charge_____ = $ _$4.00_
Subtotal _____ = $ _____
In Canada add 7% GST OR 15% HST where applicable _____ = $ _____
Total enclosed _____ = $ _____

$12.95 U.S. and international orders, payable in U.S. funds. U.S. shipping $4.00.
Price is subject to change.

NAME:_____
STREET: _____
CITY: _____ PROV./STATE _____
COUNTRY _____ POSTAL CODE/ZIP_____

Please make cheque or money order payable to:
**Pirouette Publications**
**Site 21 – 9 – RR 5**
**Prince Albert, Saskatchewan**   **Phone/Fax: (306) 764-2413**
**Canada  S6V 5R3**   **E-mail: pirouette_order@hotmail.com**
For fund raising or volume purchase prices, contact
Pirouette Publications. Please allow 3-4 weeks for delivery.

· · · · · · · · · · · · · · · · · · · · · · · · · · · · · · · · · · · · · · · · · · · · · · · · · · · · · · · ·

# Share *The Joy of Gardening* with a friend

Order *The Joy of Gardening* at $14.95 per book plus $4.00 (total order) for postage and handling.

Number of books _____ x $14.95 = $ _____
Shipping and handling charge_____ = $ _$4.00_
Subtotal _____ = $ _____
In Canada add 7% GST OR 15% HST where applicable _____ = $ _____
Total enclosed _____ = $ _____

$12.95 U.S. and international orders, payable in U.S. funds. U.S. shipping $4.00.
Price is subject to change.

NAME:_____
STREET: _____
CITY: _____ PROV./STATE _____
COUNTRY _____ POSTAL CODE/ZIP_____

Please make cheque or money order payable to:
**Pirouette Publications**
**Site 21 – 9 – RR 5**
**Prince Albert, Saskatchewan**   **Phone/Fax: (306) 764-2413**
**Canada  S6V 5R3**   **E-mail: pirouette_order@hotmail.com**
For fund raising or volume purchase prices, contact
Pirouette Publications. Please allow 3-4 weeks for delivery.

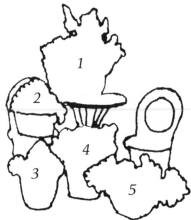